High Shelf

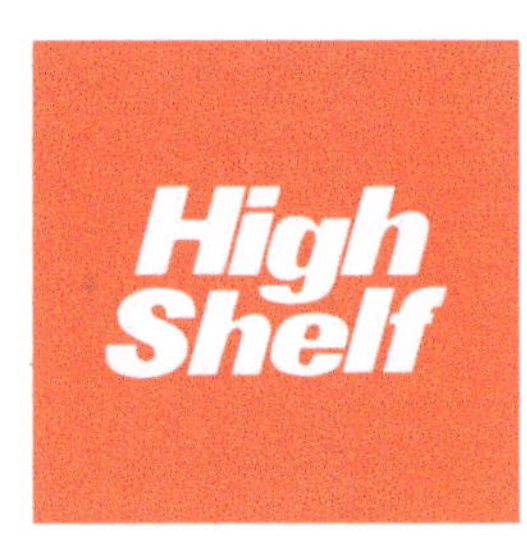

High Shelf XXXIX. February 2022.
Portland, Oregon.
Copyright 2022, High Shelf Press

ISBN: 978-1-952869-56-3

Cover Image by Jamie Parks
Editing, Design and Layout by C. M. Tollefson

With special thanks to:
David Seung & Eric Hoskins

High Shelf XXXXIX

February 2022

"... A bang on the door. My neighbor asks to borrow my car.
At this hour, he may or may not be sober,... "
Devon Balwit

"... who are we to talk about cages
of steel and concrete?

Can the creature unlatch itself? Use the imagination..."
Anthony J. Dennis

Table Of Contents

MORE STUBBORN THAN THE SEA — 9
Mitch Rayes

Where the secrets are — 1C
Jamie Parks

Bankrupt — 12
Iumi Richard-Crow

some photos — 15
George L Stein

Mere/ness — 3C
Saleem Abdal-Khaaliq

Raising a Ruckus — 31
Devon Balwit

The Transparent Self-Disclosure/Contentment I,II,III, Dntbafrd, CupidsPsyche II — 3:
Planta Vilar

Animals under the Sun — 4:
Anthony J. Dennis

My Struggle — 4:
Andrea Lee Dunn

Kids Don't Sound That Great To Me — 4:
Grace Dilger

L A G T I ME — 4:
Kimberly Kradel

The Nitrous Dealer's Beautiful Wife — 5C
Christopher Norcross

Folie A Deux — 5:
Mac Chandler

Florence in Motion — 5:
John Lightle

Citrus and Asbestos: The Tale of Amos — 7.
Sam Waldron

The Agent's Critique   76
N.M. Campbell

The Workman Way   82
Fred Pierre

Ekphrastic Challenge   88
Eric Walker & Isobel Rossiter

MORE STUBBORN THAN THE SEA

Mitch Rayes

we are superimposed upon layers of time
this sidewalk is a disturbance in a desert that used to be an ocean

we are its fish who've lost the ability to navigate or breathe
abandoned even by the elements we were evolved to inhabit

perhaps we each hold something the other needs to know

but all that's left of the ocean is a fish bowl between my ears
where your shadow moves furtively
unable to speak

Where the secrets are

Jamie Parks

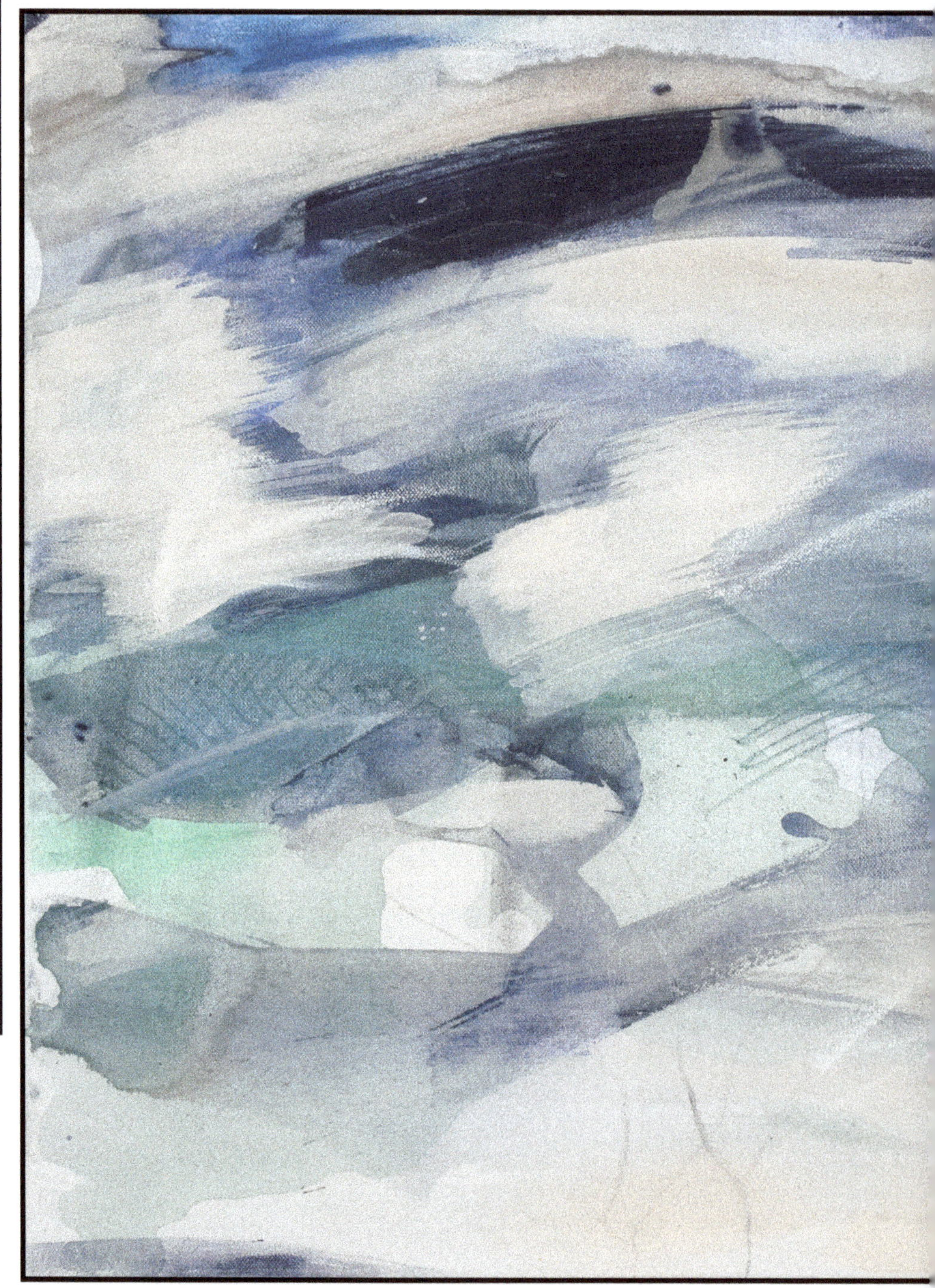

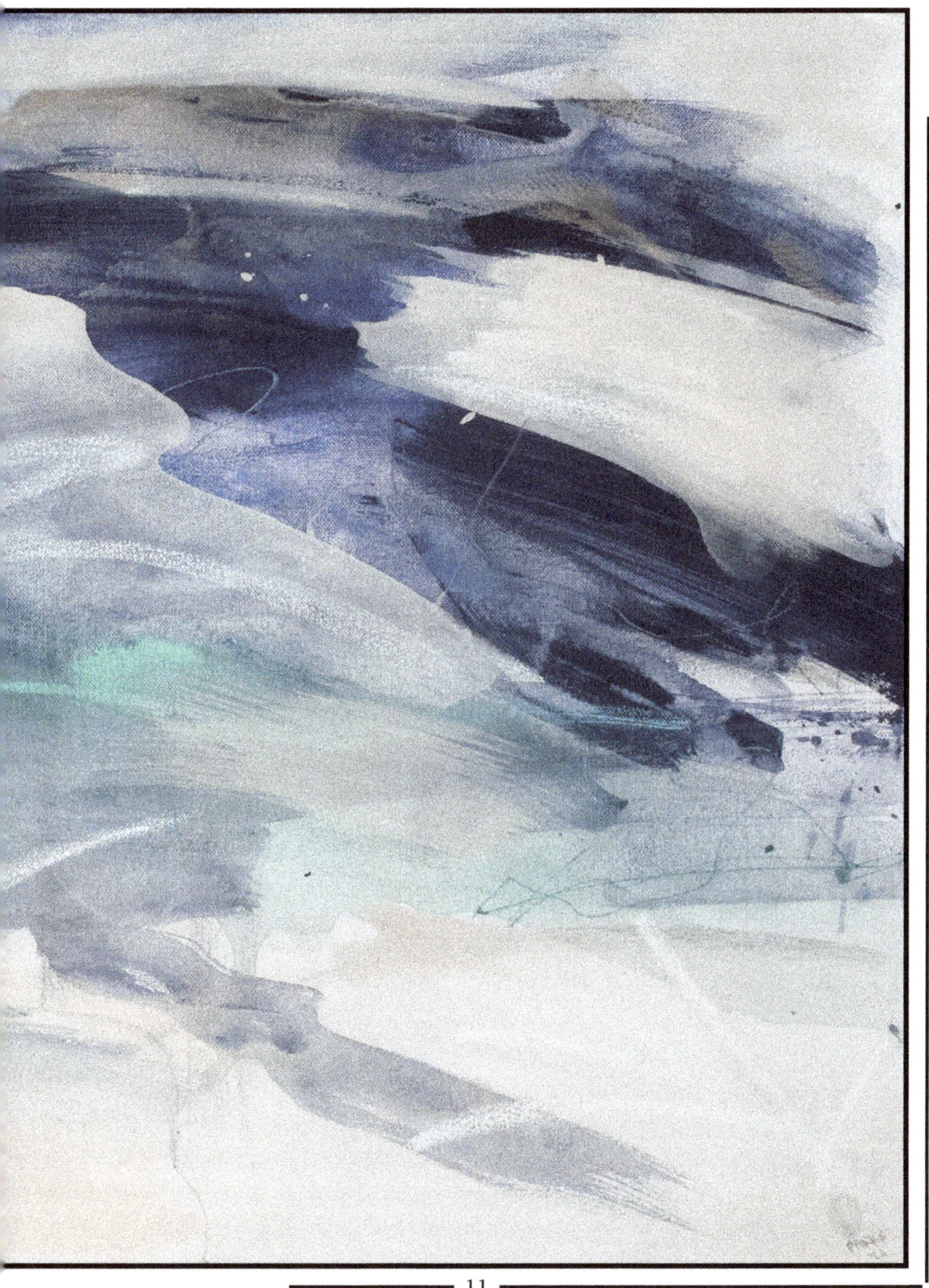

Bankrupt

Iumi Richard-Crow

We think, you and I, that we can escape
the underbelly of love.
That is, ward off the heartache.

We think we can avoid
the back pages of wandering.
The being lost.

We run clumsy like weekend warriors in dubious marathons
on mornings closed in on themselves.
We careen unfazed through confused alleyways
leading to neighborhoods
lined with barbed wire and rimmed with signs that bark
Keep Out.
Signs that growl
No TrustPassing.

We think, you and I, that we can evade
the failings of lovers.
That is, fend off the bitterness.

We take trips to struggling retreats, replete with all-you-can eat.
Cavernous barns crowded
with the disenchanted, determined
to feast a path to forgetting.
We join them at the buffet,
every item capsized in grease,
dredged in sawdust.

The soft blue mist casts shadows on the hearth.
The soft blue rain overcomes the heat
and wishes it was fire, cries
and turns into steam
cries and evaporates.

There is no time to linger.
We go to bed hungry
in rooms where widows weep.

We think, you and I, that we can avert
the torpor of familiarity.

That is, shake off the boredom.

There is no time to linger. No time for give and take.
We will not pause to contemplate our weary,
sometimes lively,
always uncertain fate.
No time for chatter.
No time to sweep up the glass that shatters,
cheerfully thrown,
drunkenly dropped.

No time to linger.
We go to bed thirsty
in rooms where widows weep.

We think, you and I, that we can deflect
the gossip of failure.
That is, fake out the disappointment.

No time left for worry or regrets. Time is the train
we missed, the lover we failed to meet.
We leave time and station,
give away our ration of self-reflection
to the panhandler whose sign assures,
"anything will help."

In haste we drop our bags, squander what binds us.
Misspend memories. Surrender symbols that define us.
Alone together, we glimpse faces speeding by,
reflections in vast windows
we do not recognize
as our own.

 No time to linger.
We go to bed lonely
in rooms where widows weep.

We lose what we lost, forget what we dropped in haste.
The sweet taste
turned tart. The waste
from our impoverished relating litters the lives of strangers.
A fragment here.
A fragment there.
A whispered shout.
An abandoned song playing out of nowhere

into someone's somewhere.

No time to linger
We go to bed solo
in rooms where widows weep.

some photos

George L Stein

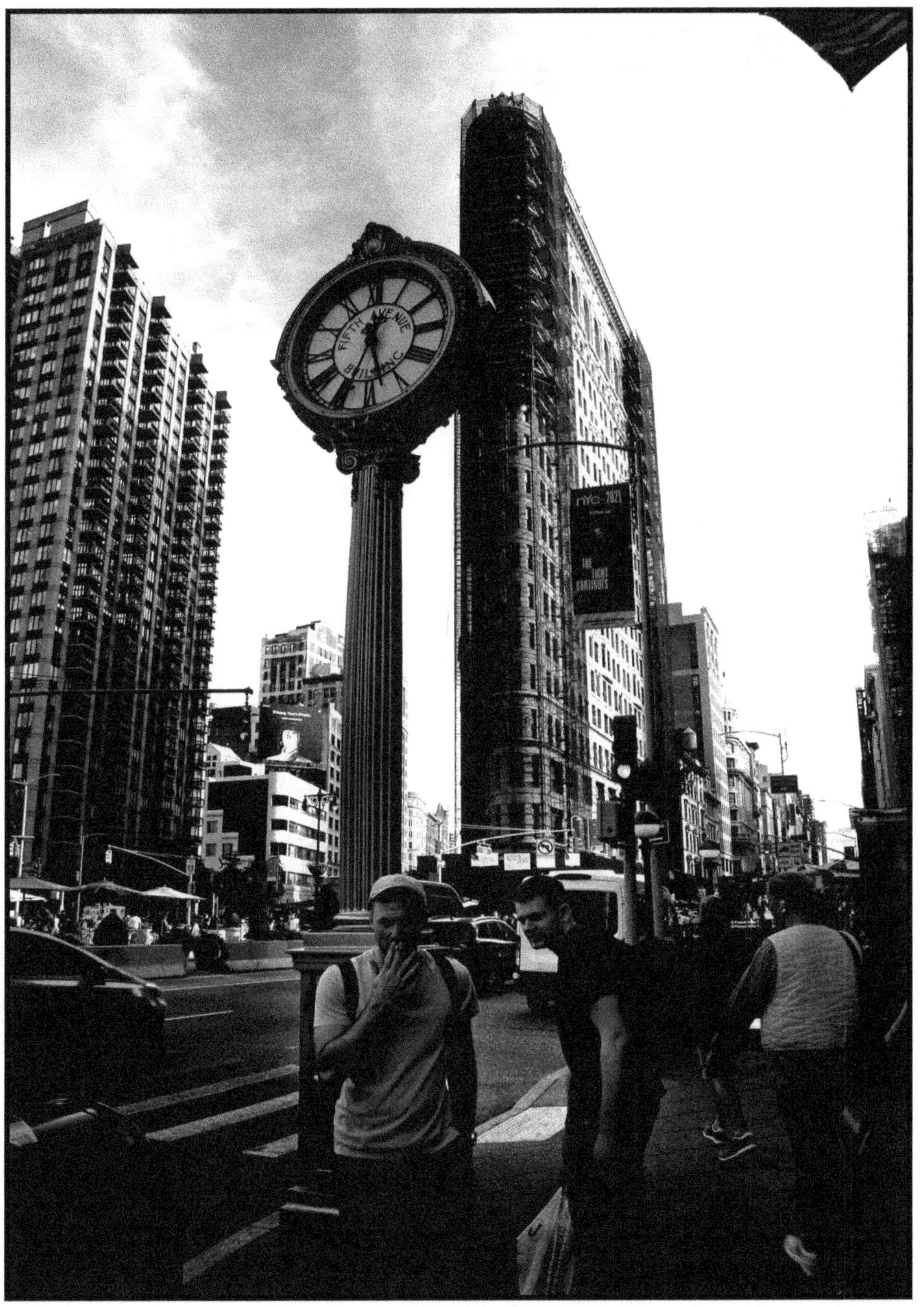

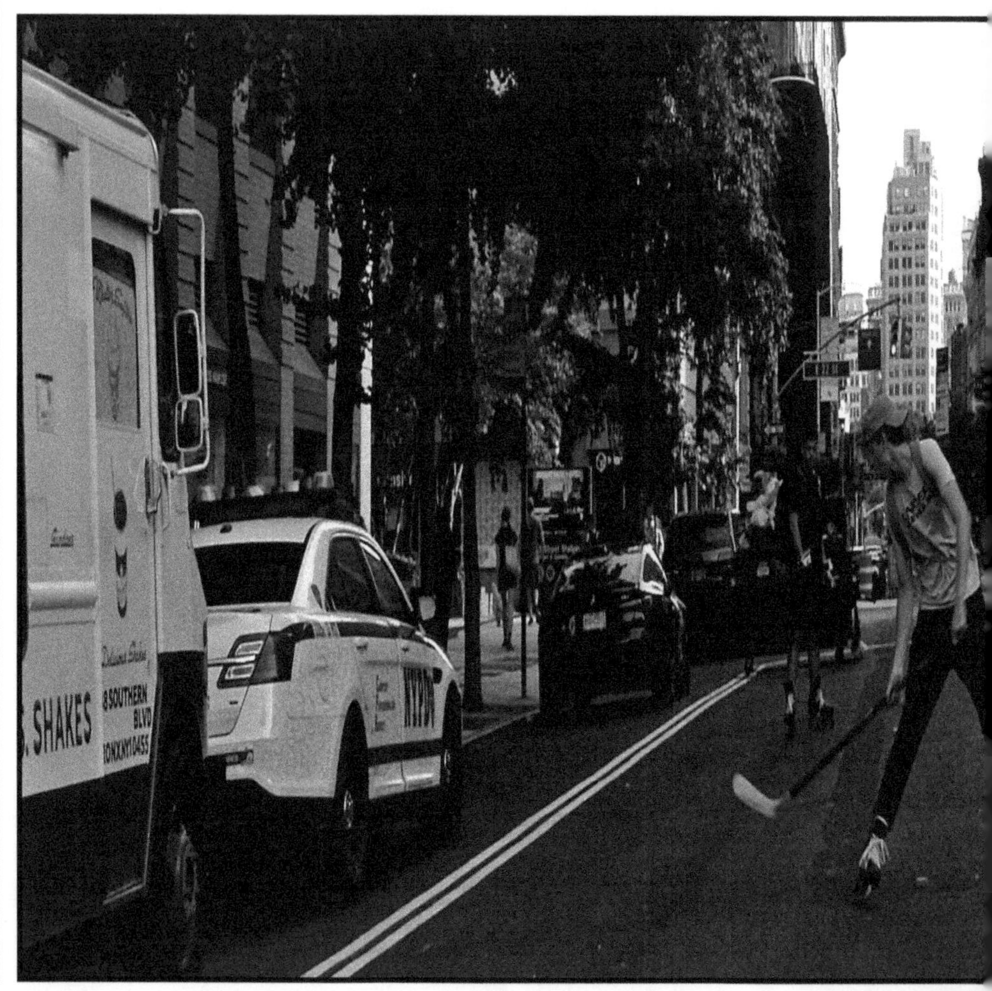
SHAKES
8 SOUTHERN
BLVD
BRONX NY 10455
NYPD

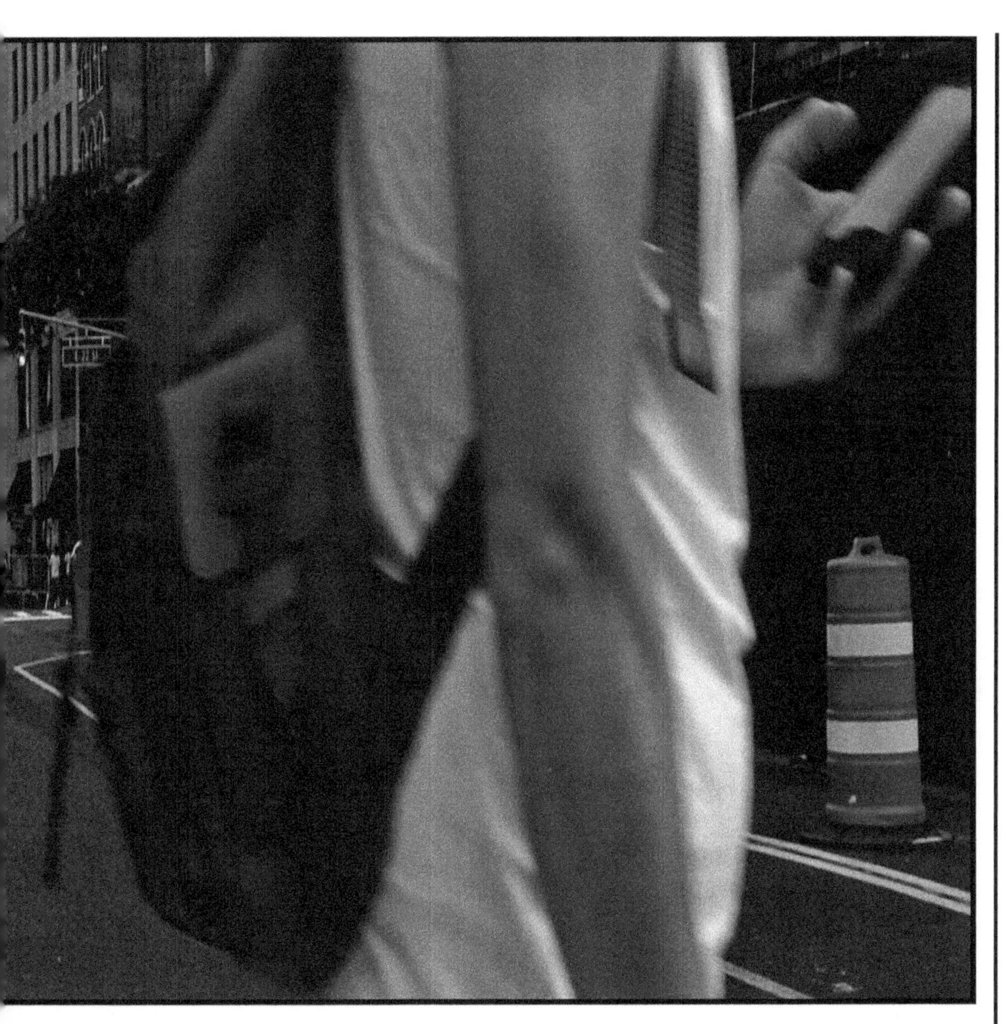

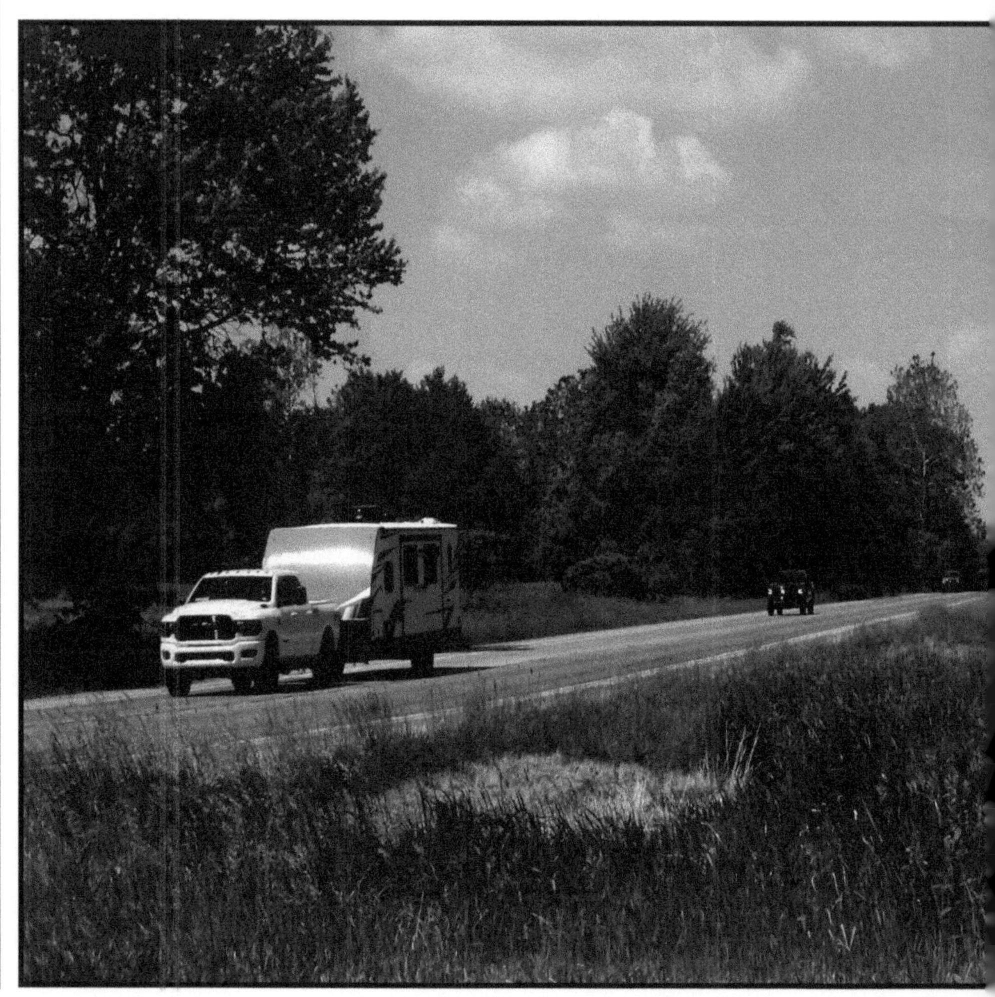

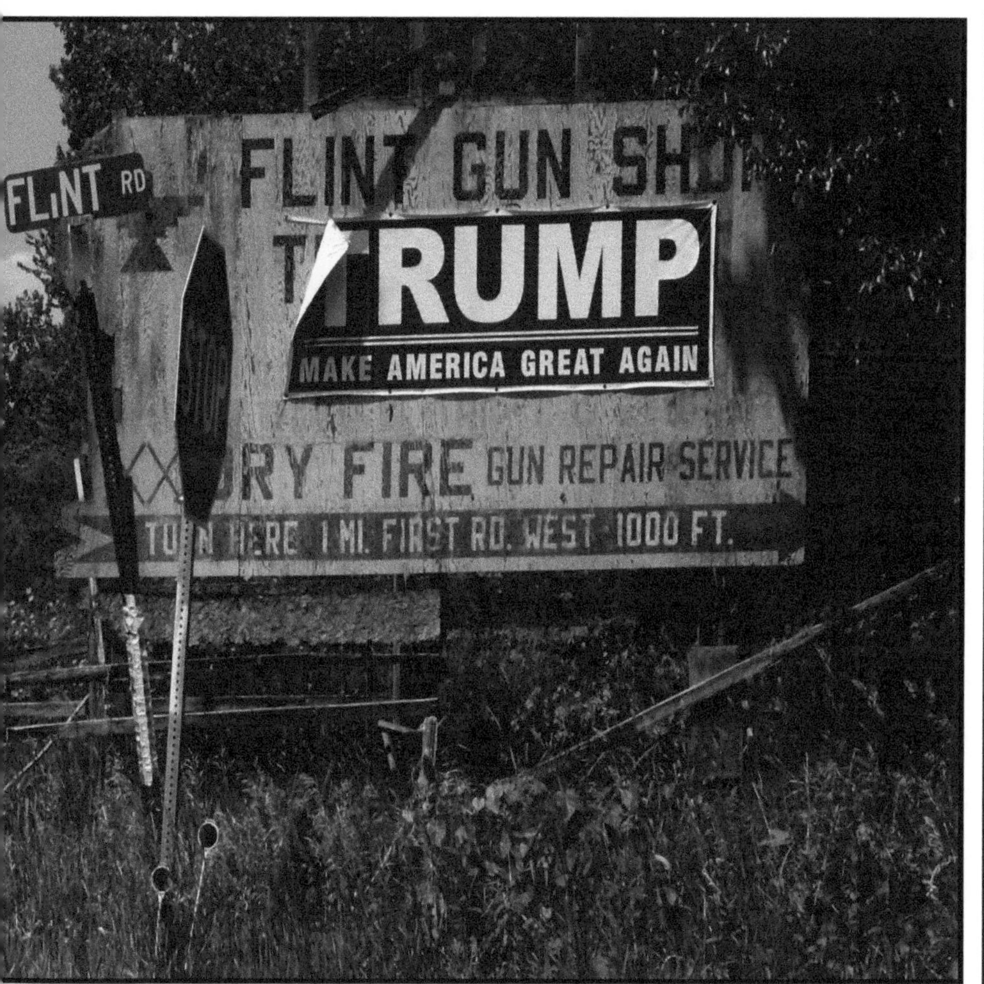

FLINT RD
FLINT
FLINT GUN SHOP
TRUMP
MAKE AMERICA GREAT AGAIN
RY FIRE GUN REPAIR SERVICE
TURN HERE 1 MI. FIRST RD. WEST 1000 FT.

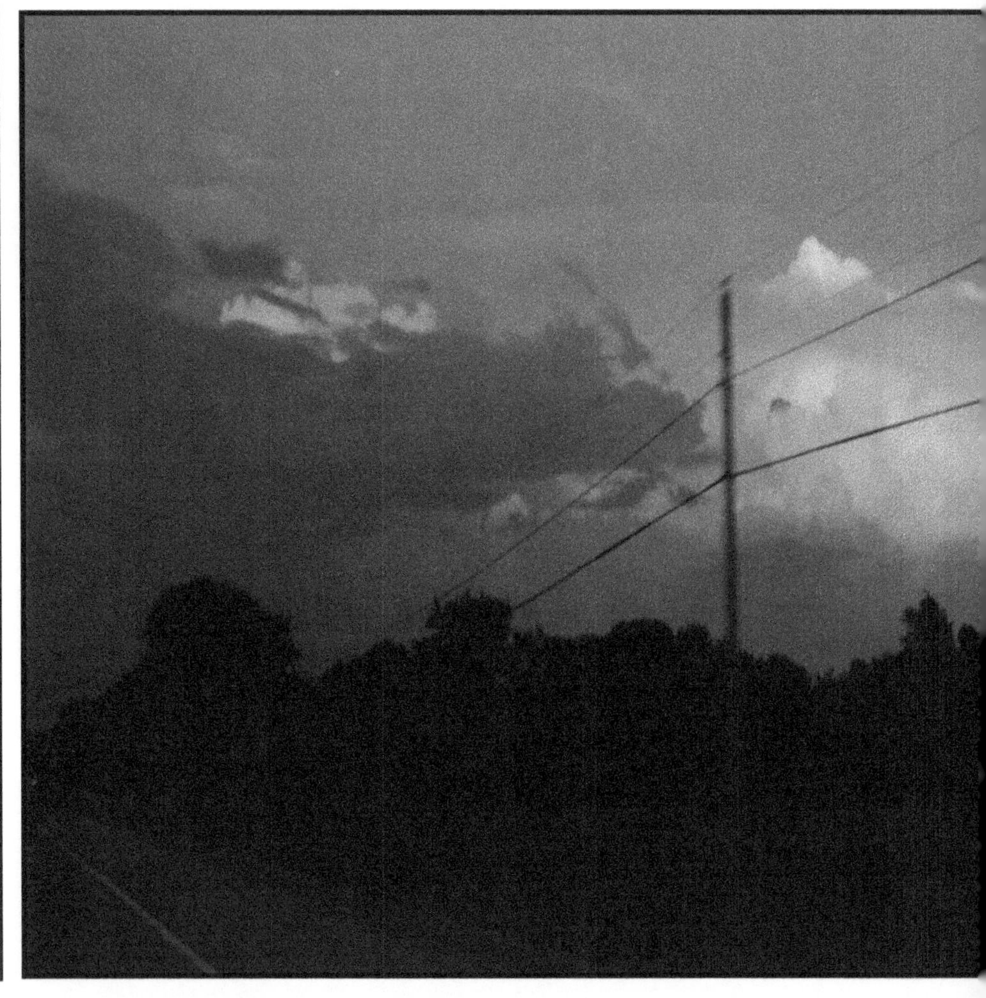

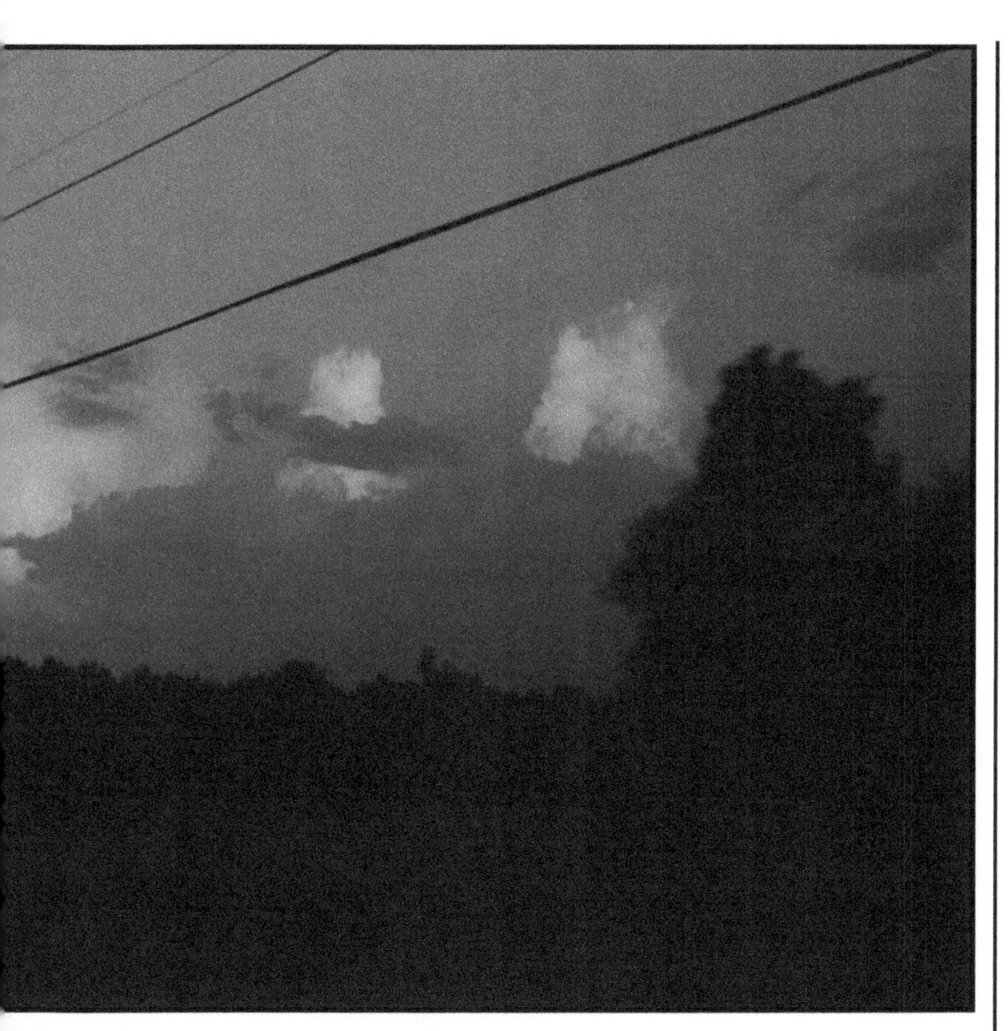

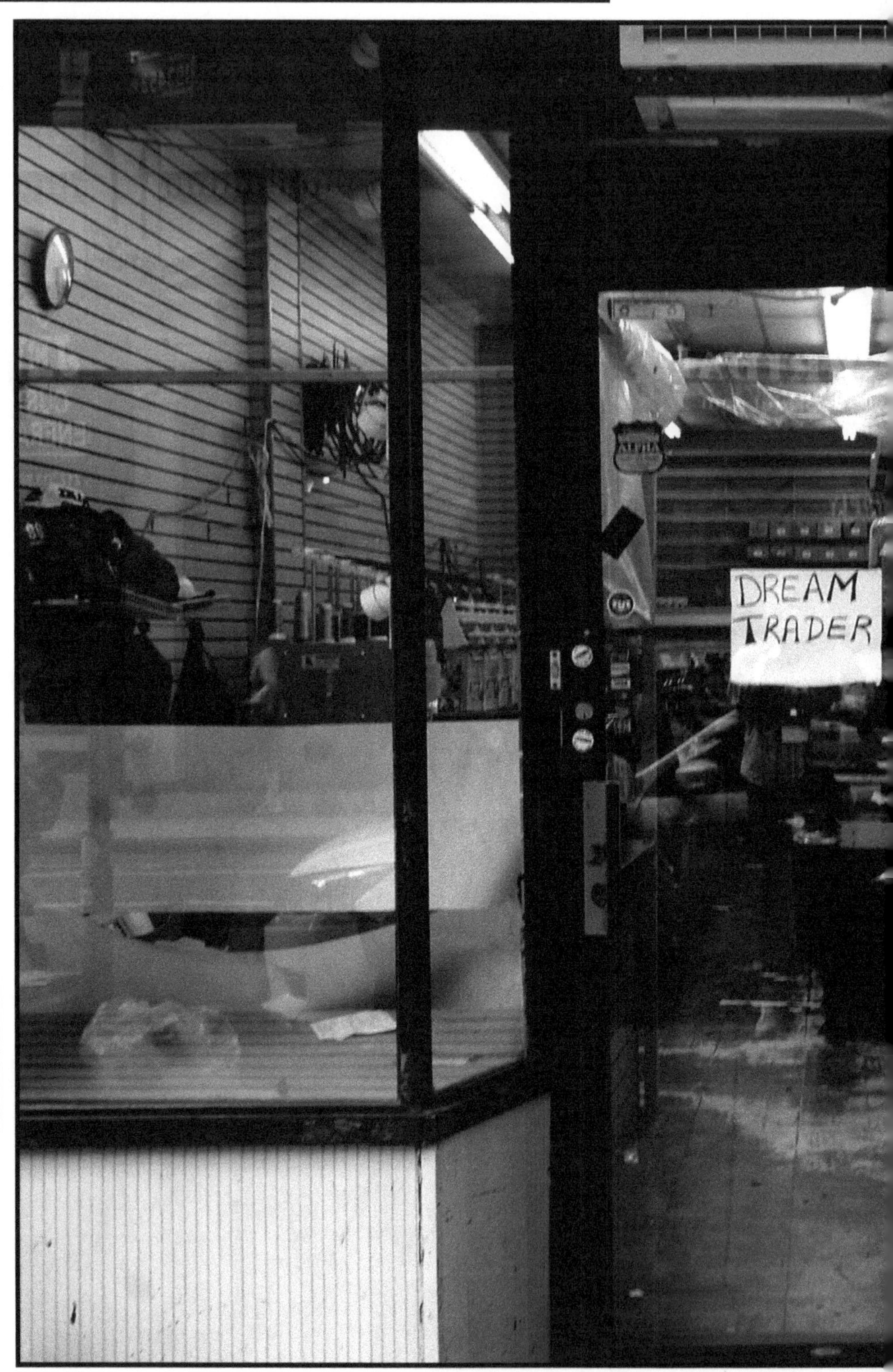
DREAM
TRADER

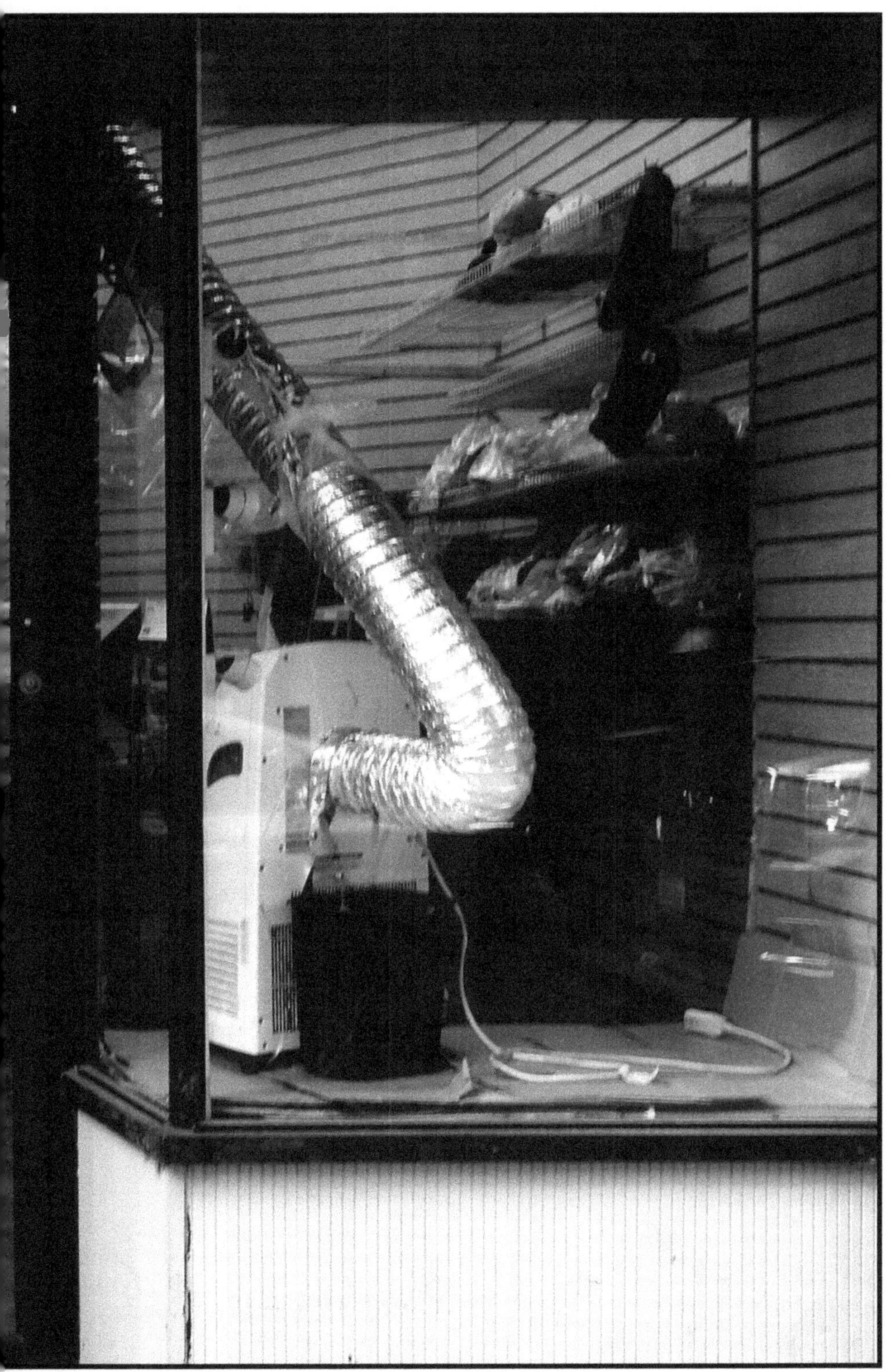

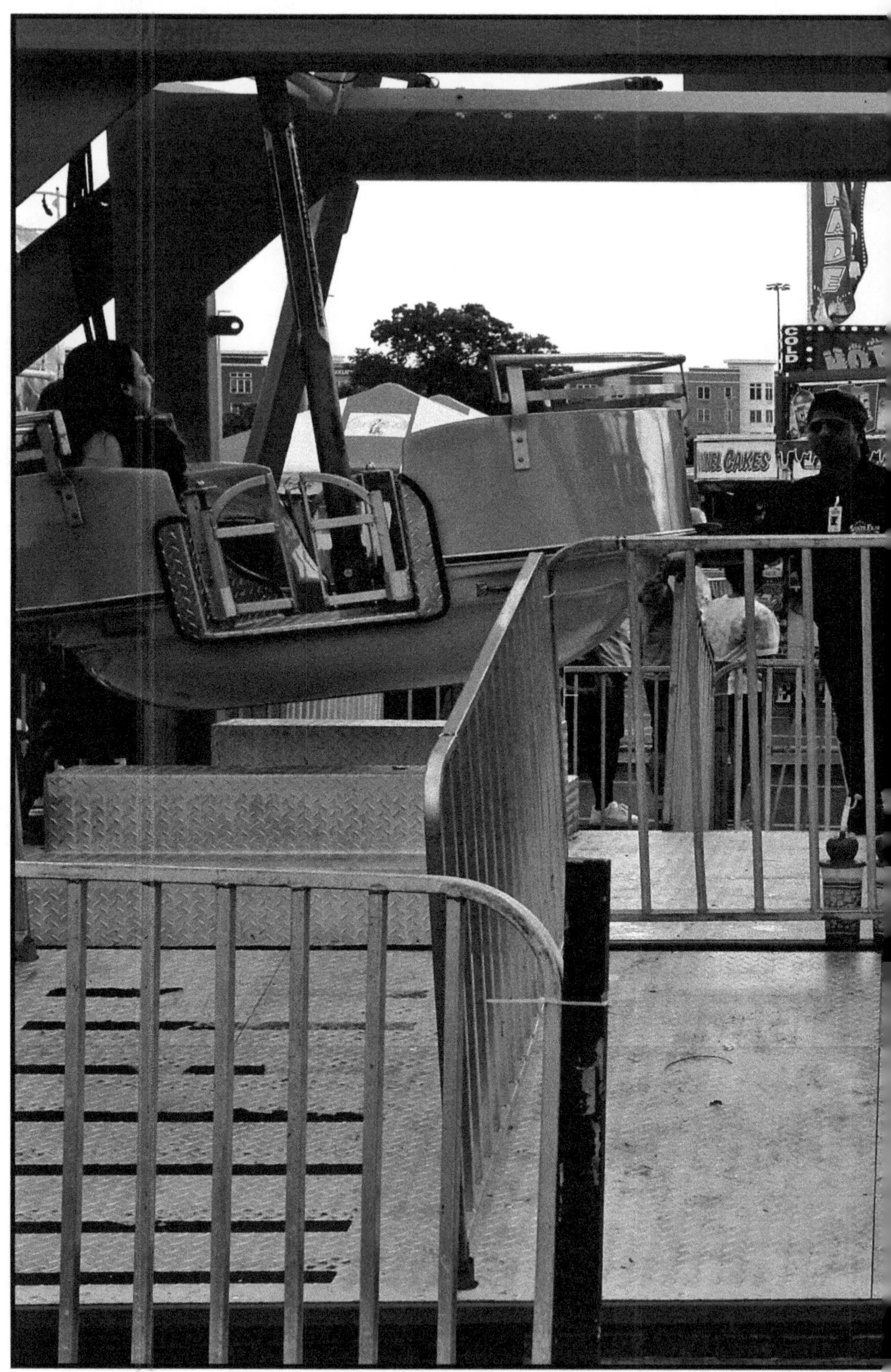

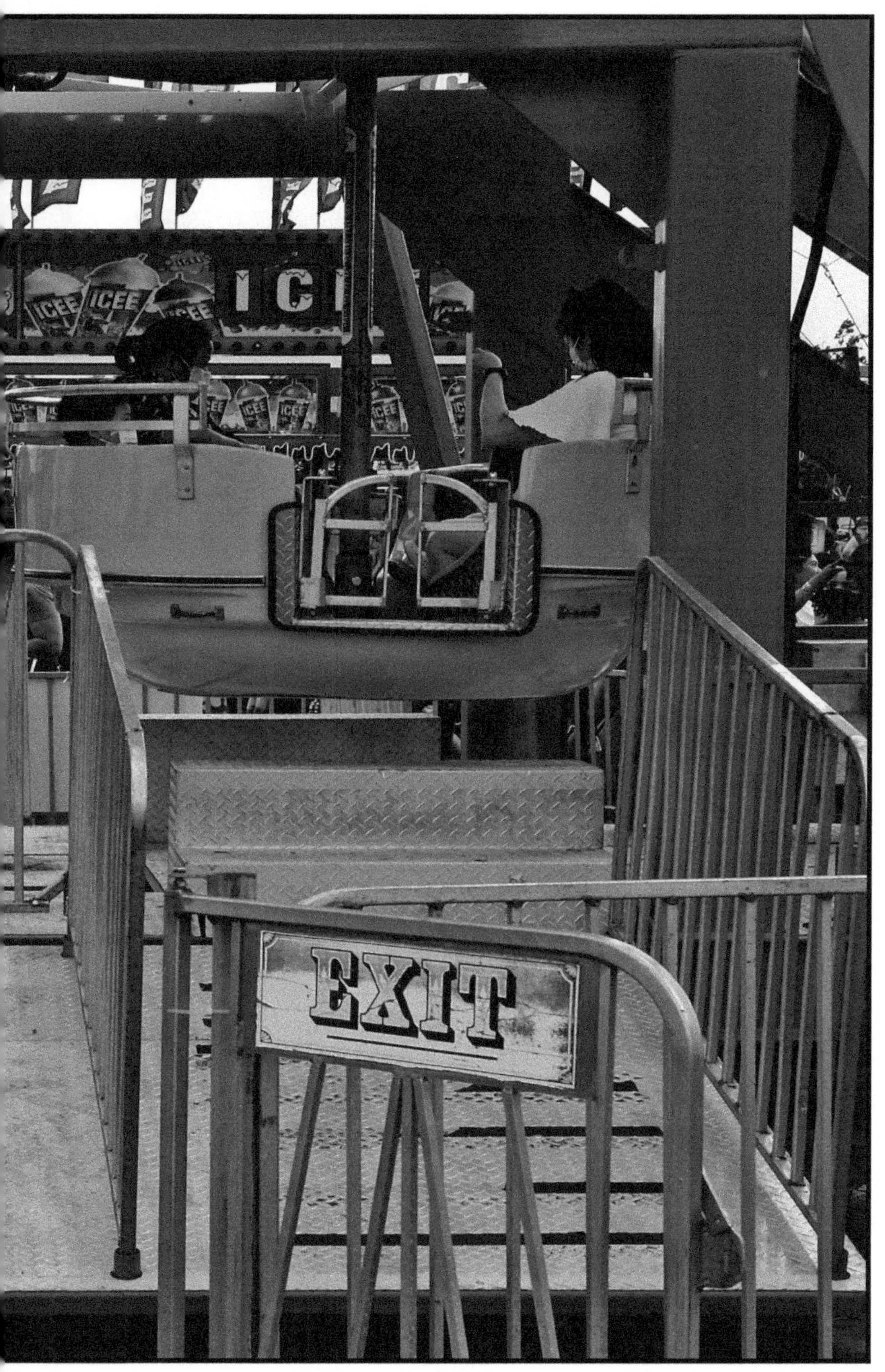

ICEE
ICEE
ICEE
ICEE
EXIT

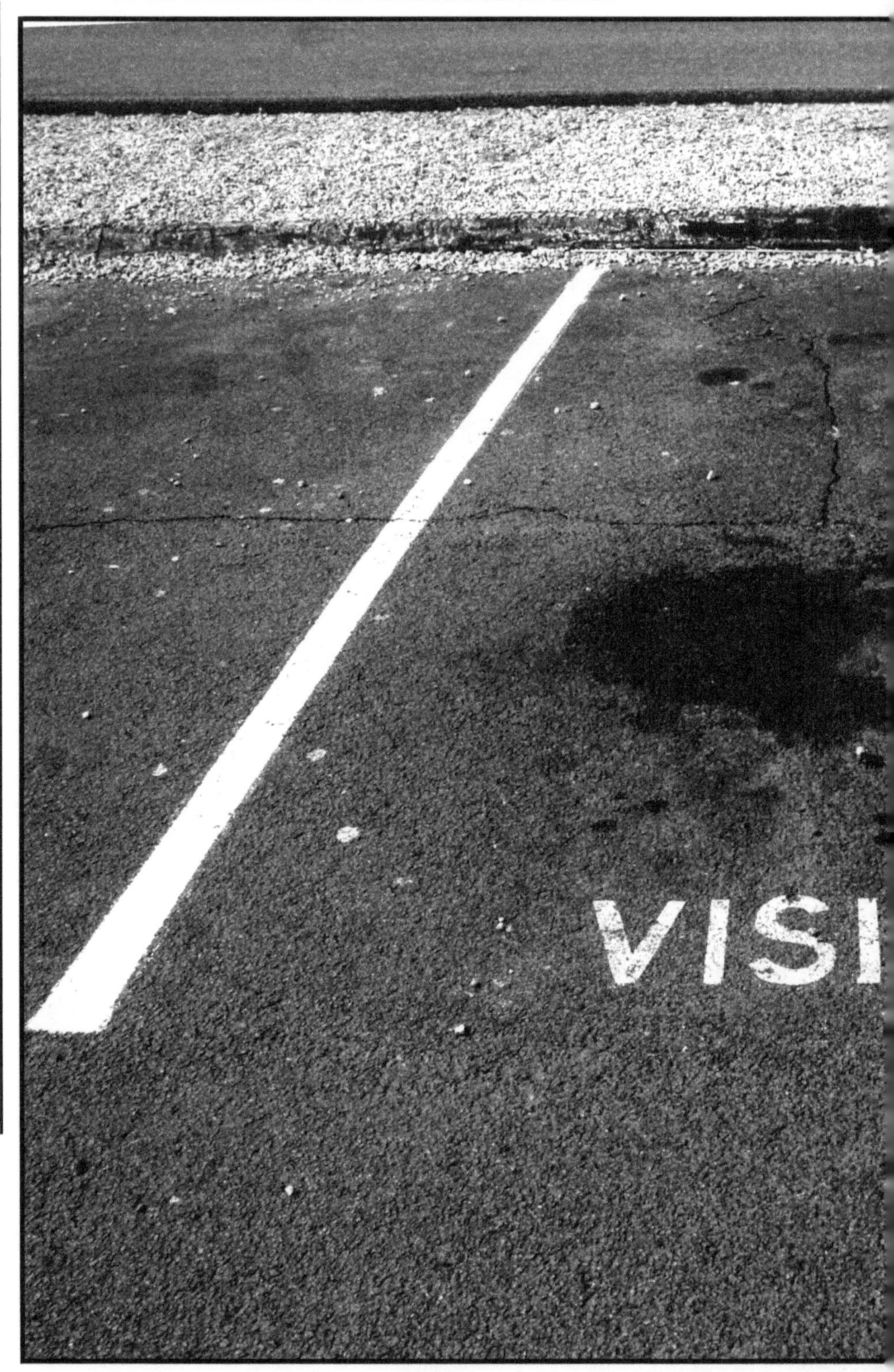
VISI

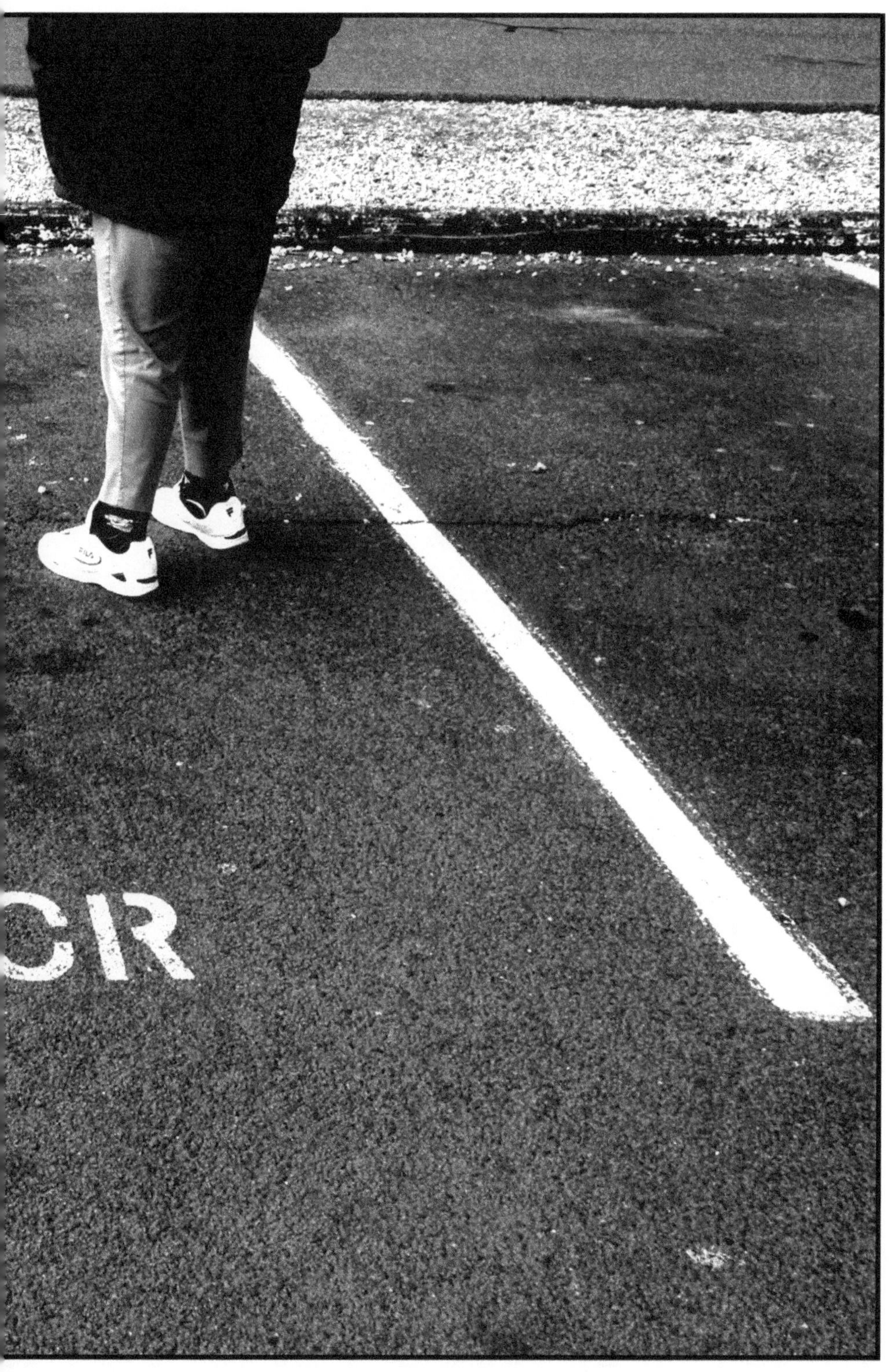

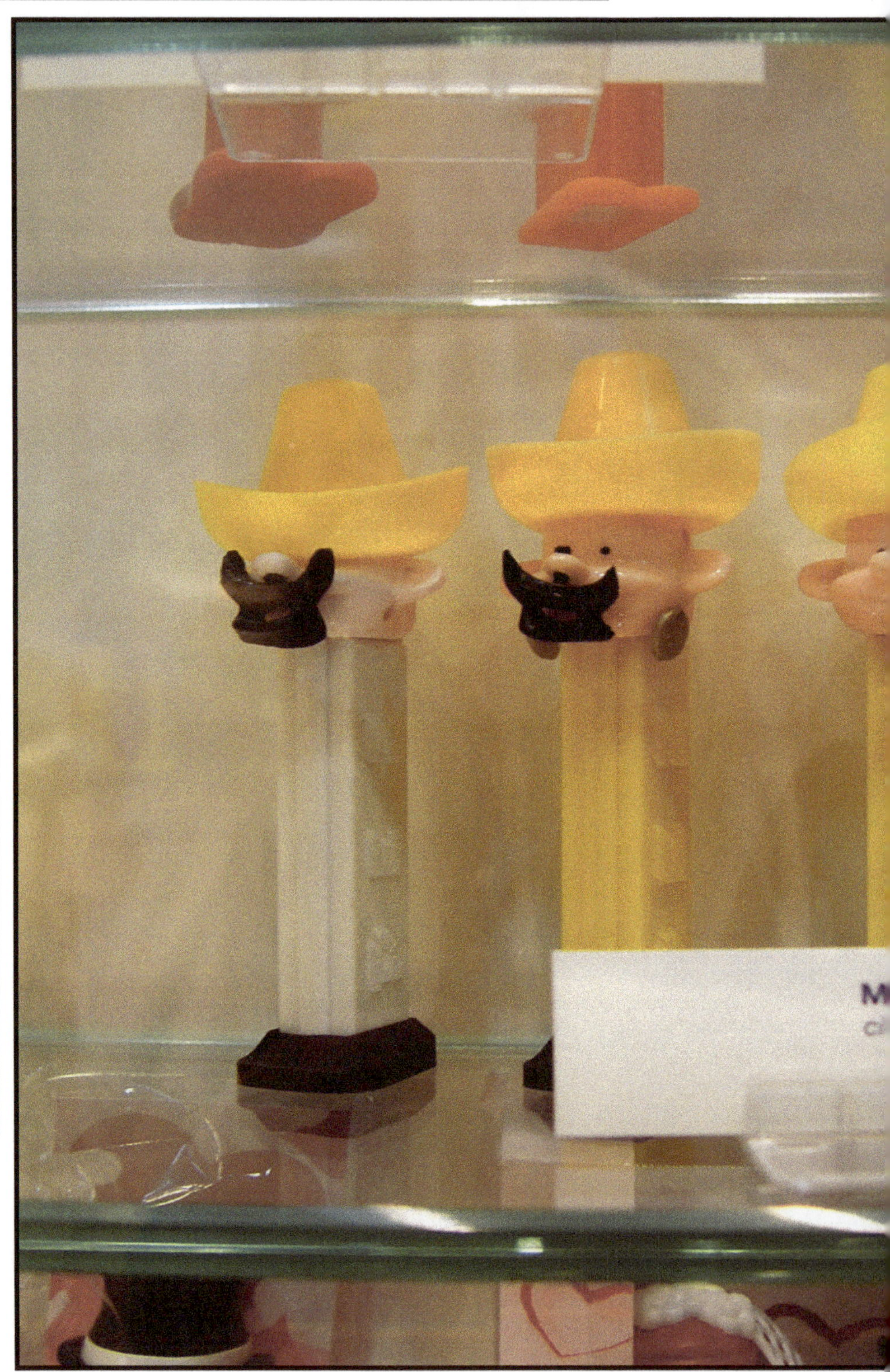

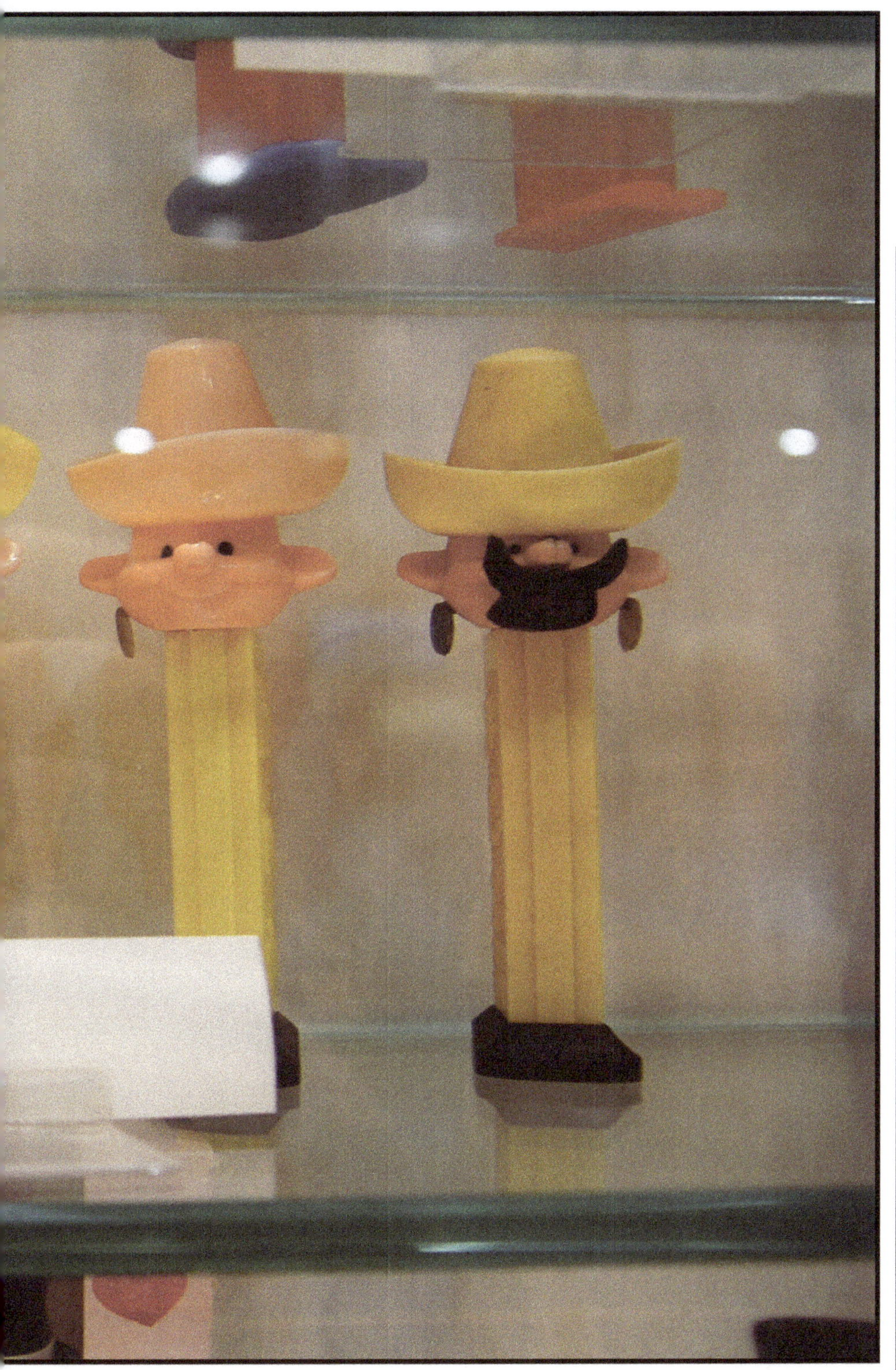

Mere/ness

Saleem Abdal-Khaaliq

The Moon is not yet full

daffodils and dandelions

dance to cull a cacophony

of mirrored yellow waves

Though the Moon is not full

a breath takes in light to

a newborn baby's heart

and spells beginning

into this starless night

There is monsoon laughter

awash everywhere

Cresting shimmering/

glitter into its air

of fractal fragrance

laced among the moon's

fabric of non-fullness

Raising a Ruckus

Devon Balwit

A bang on the door. My neighbor asks to borrow my car.
At this hour, he may or may not be sober,

but I'm a pal, and he lived here
long before me. What the hell—it's clear

he's got something urgent to do,
something about checking the view

from a maybe-apartment for after
he vacates the house, handing it over

to his ex, whose father's
money bought it. I think of the condors

lining a deck in Tehachapi after trashing the place,
asserting their rights by shitting, indelible feces

everywhere you looked. To be fair,
they foul themselves as a kind of temperature

control. *Urohidrosis*, it's called. I can relate
to such self-management, the fate

of our body locked to that of our head—
my neighbor who cranks his stereo, ready

to howl all night until muted by dawn. The condors
are tagged with mugshot numbers. An augur

might buy a lottery ticket in just that order.
I, however, won't bet on my neighbor.

The Transparent Self-Disclosure/Contentment I,II,III, Dntbafrd, CupidsPsyche II

Planta Vilar

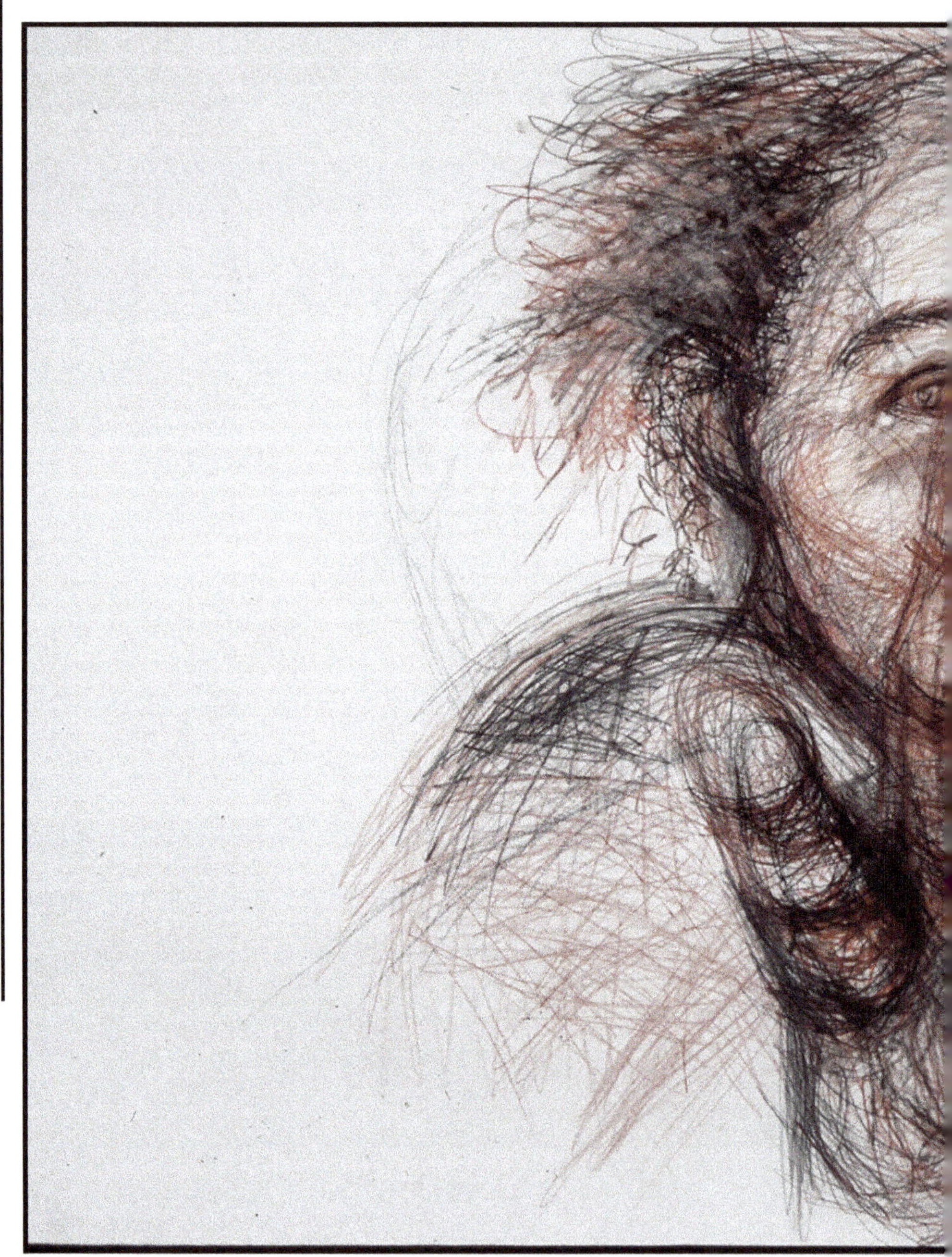

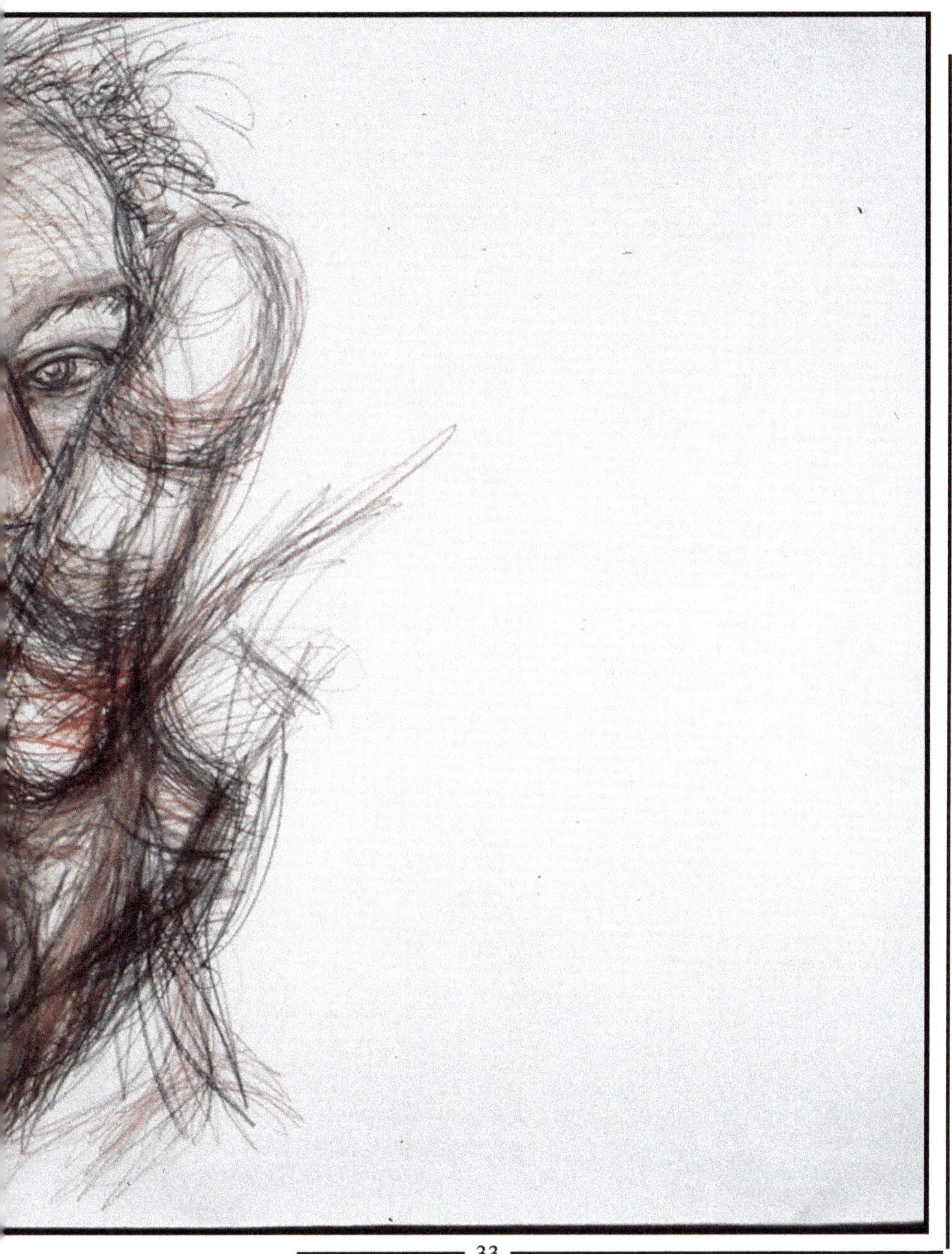

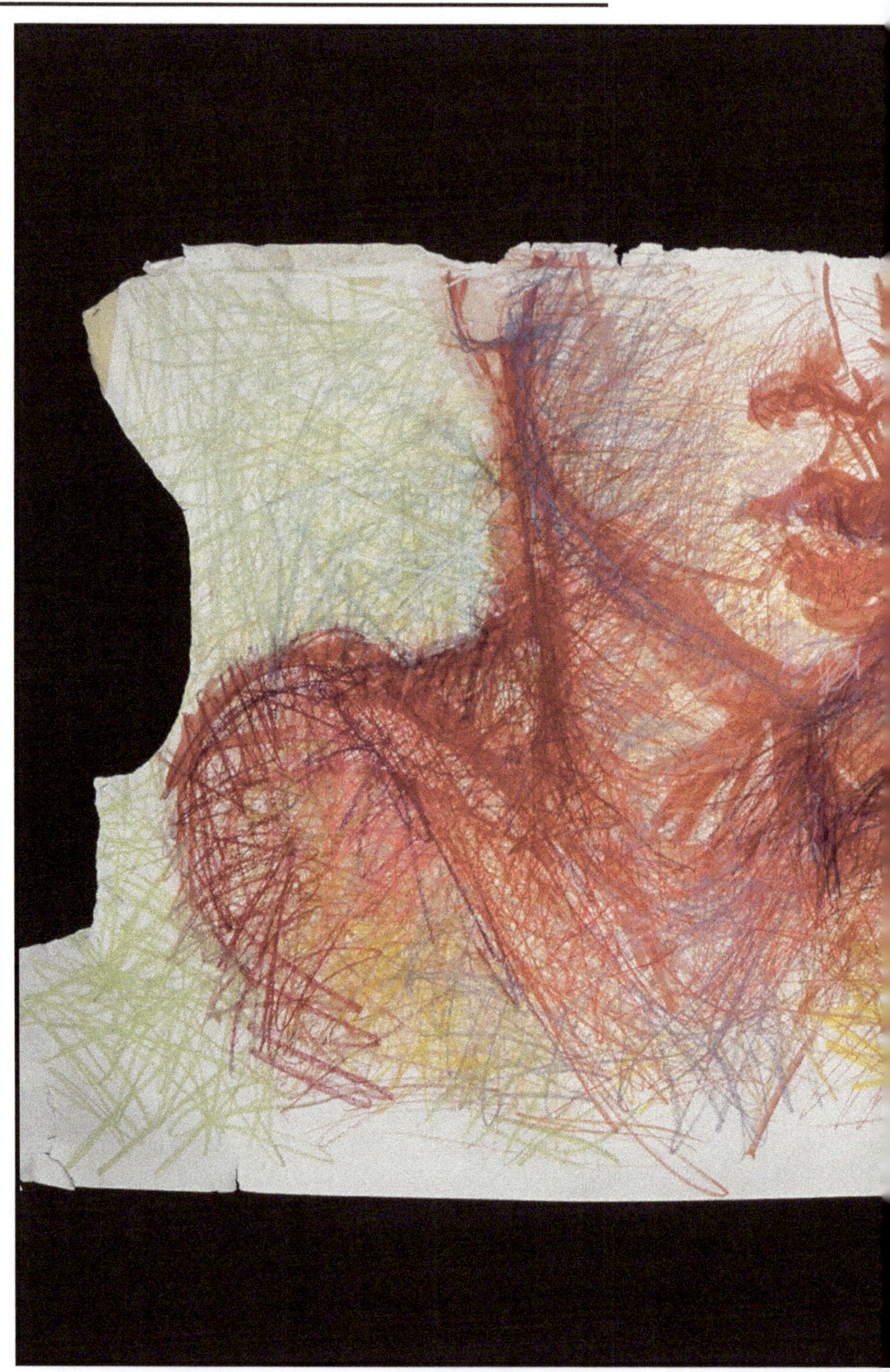

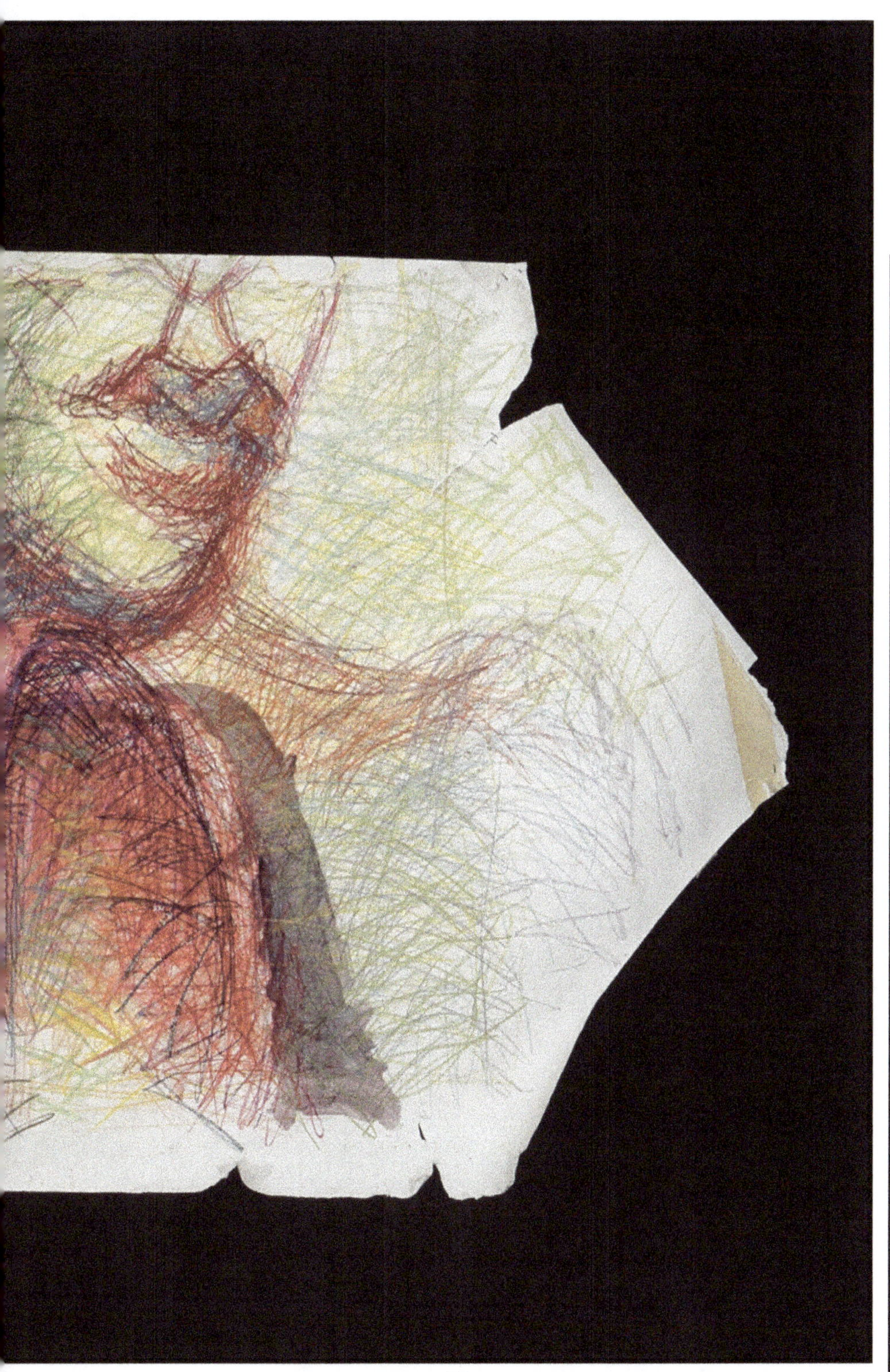

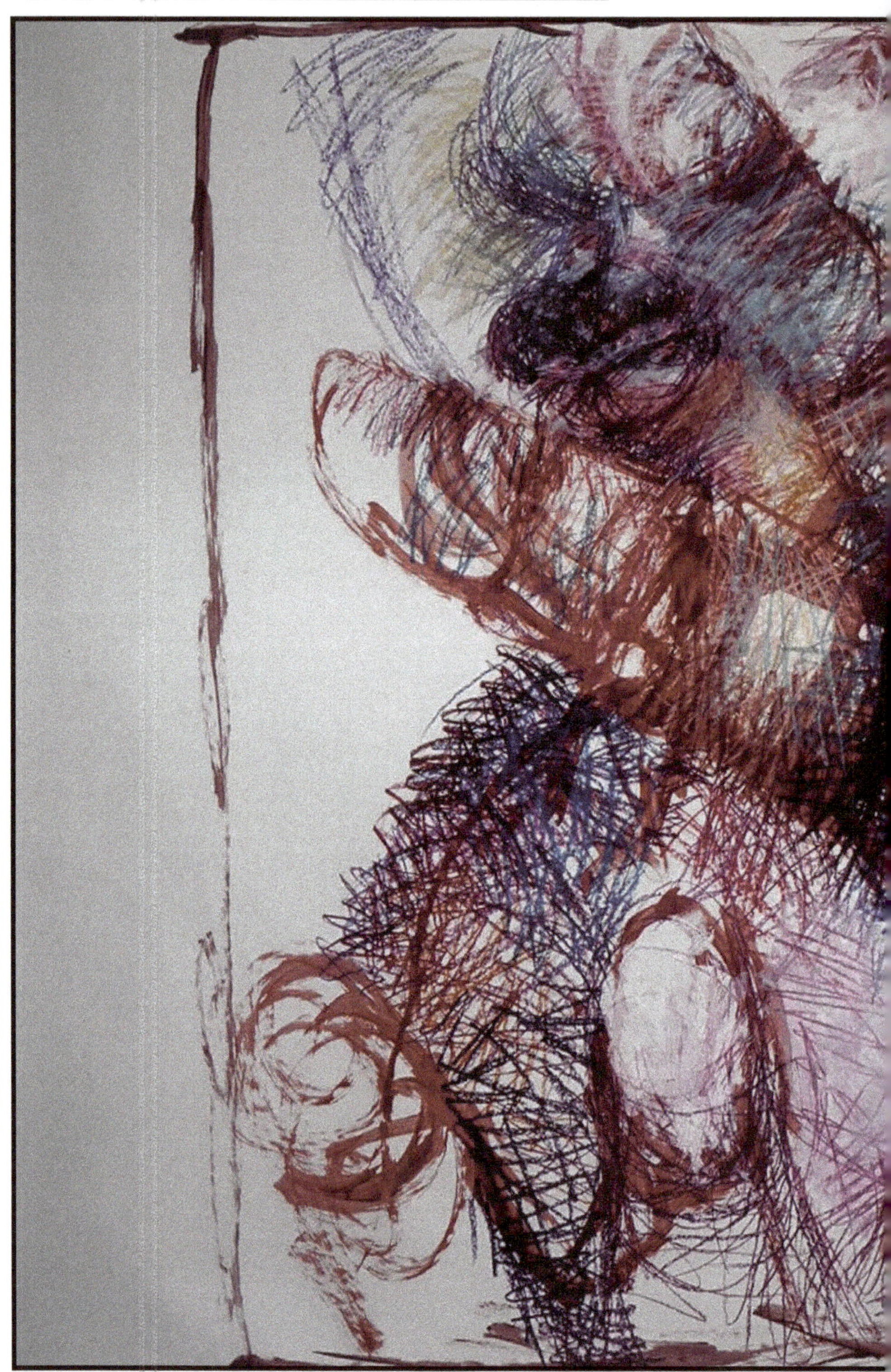

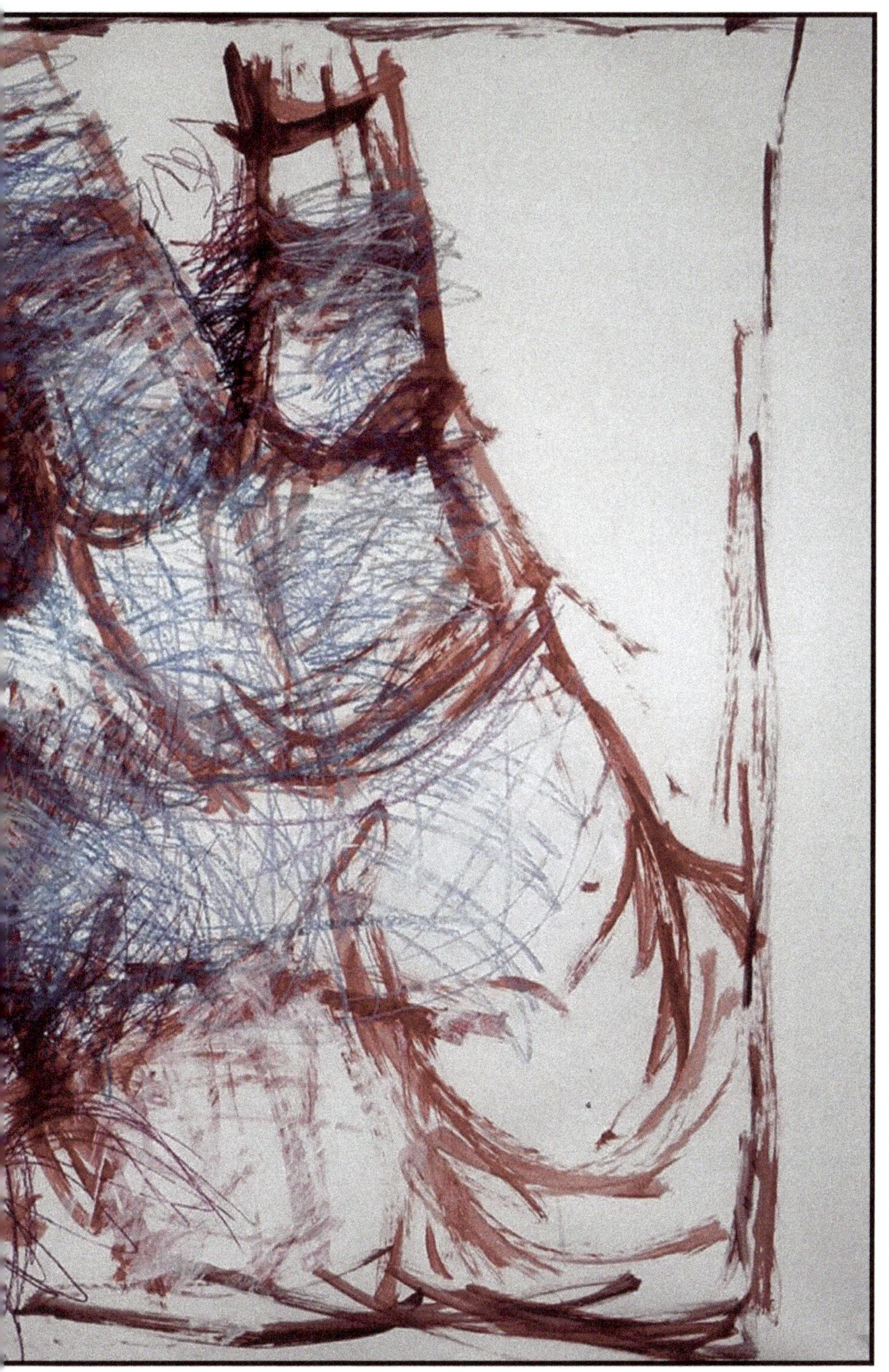

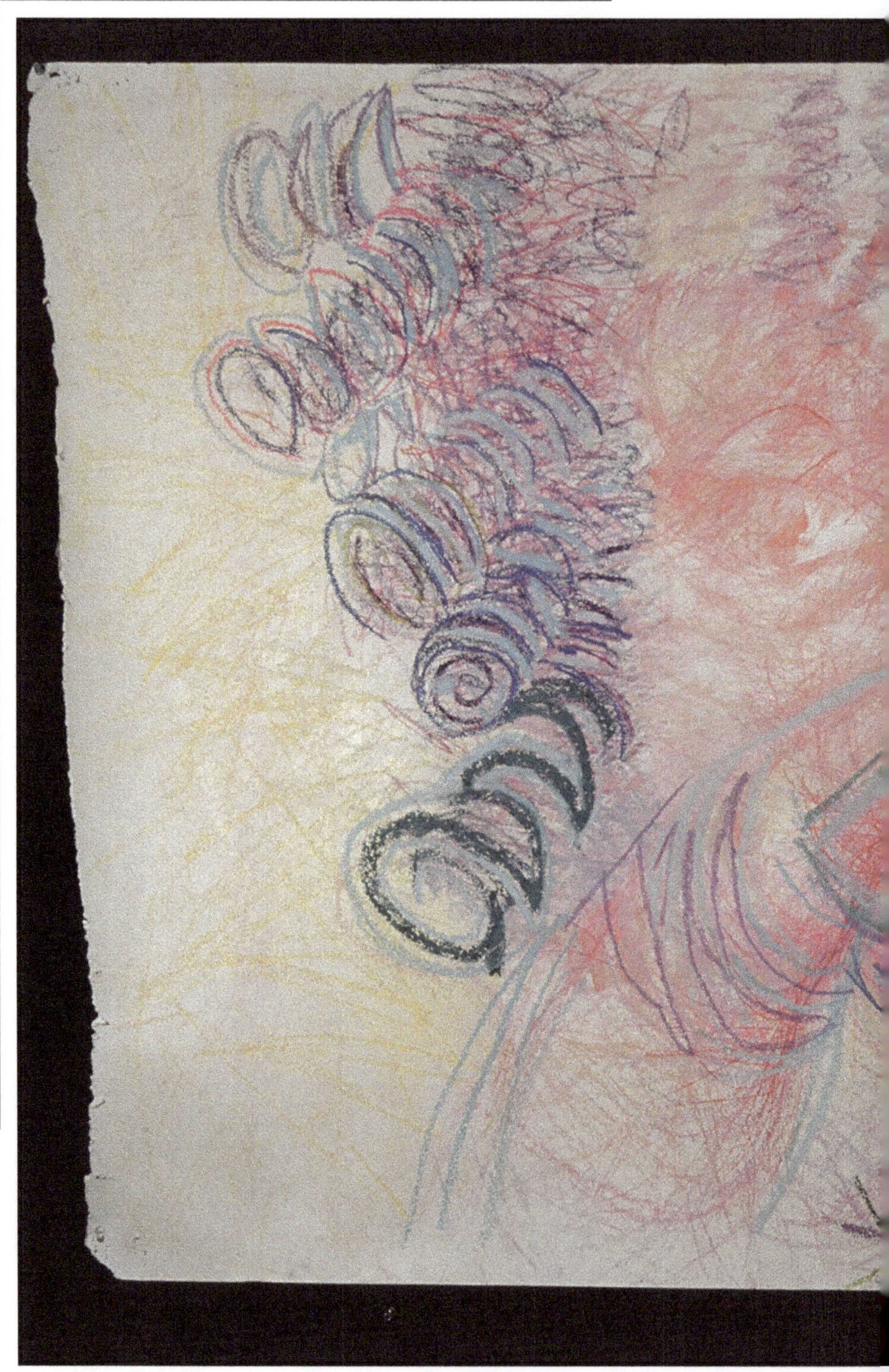

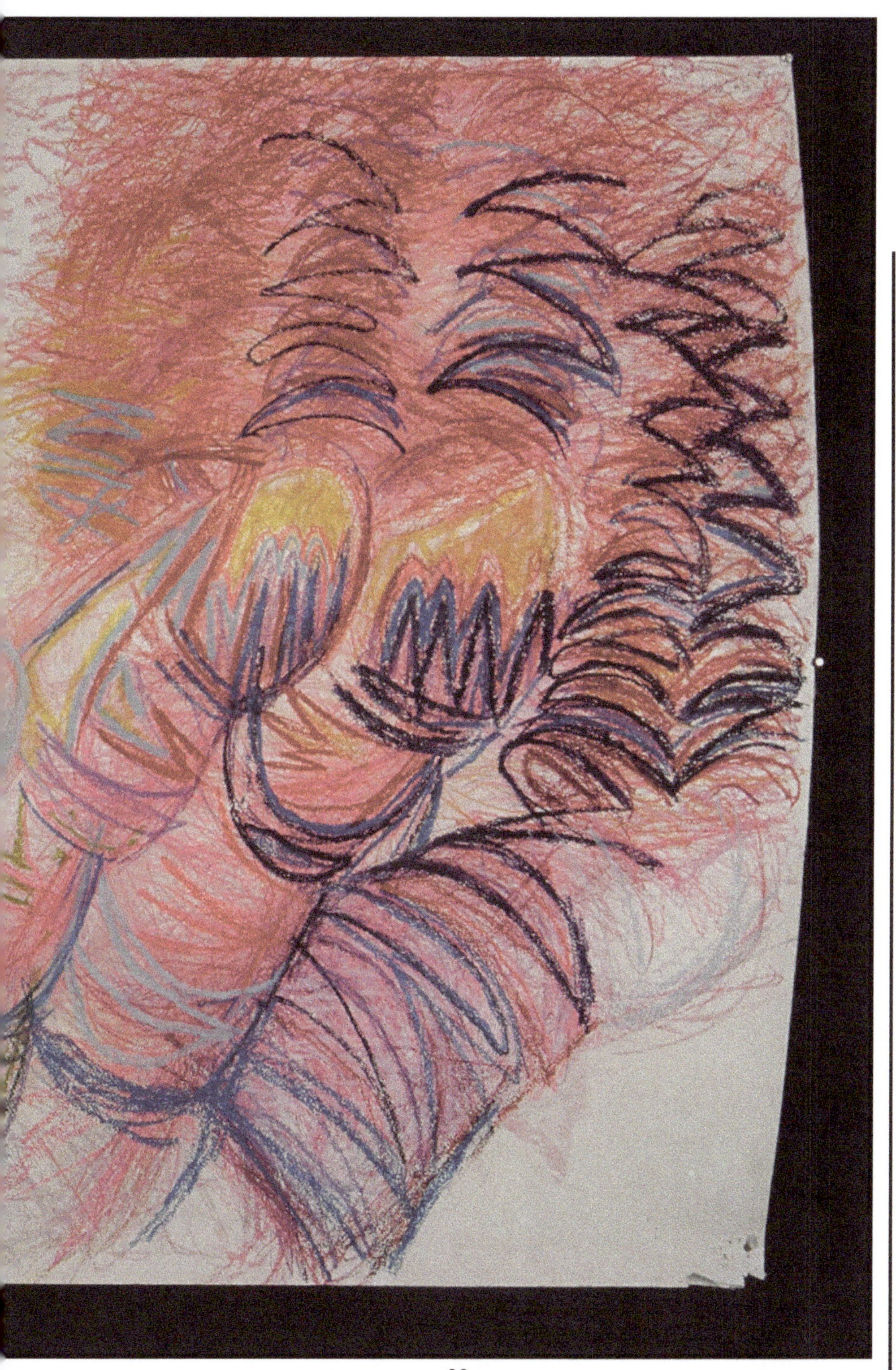

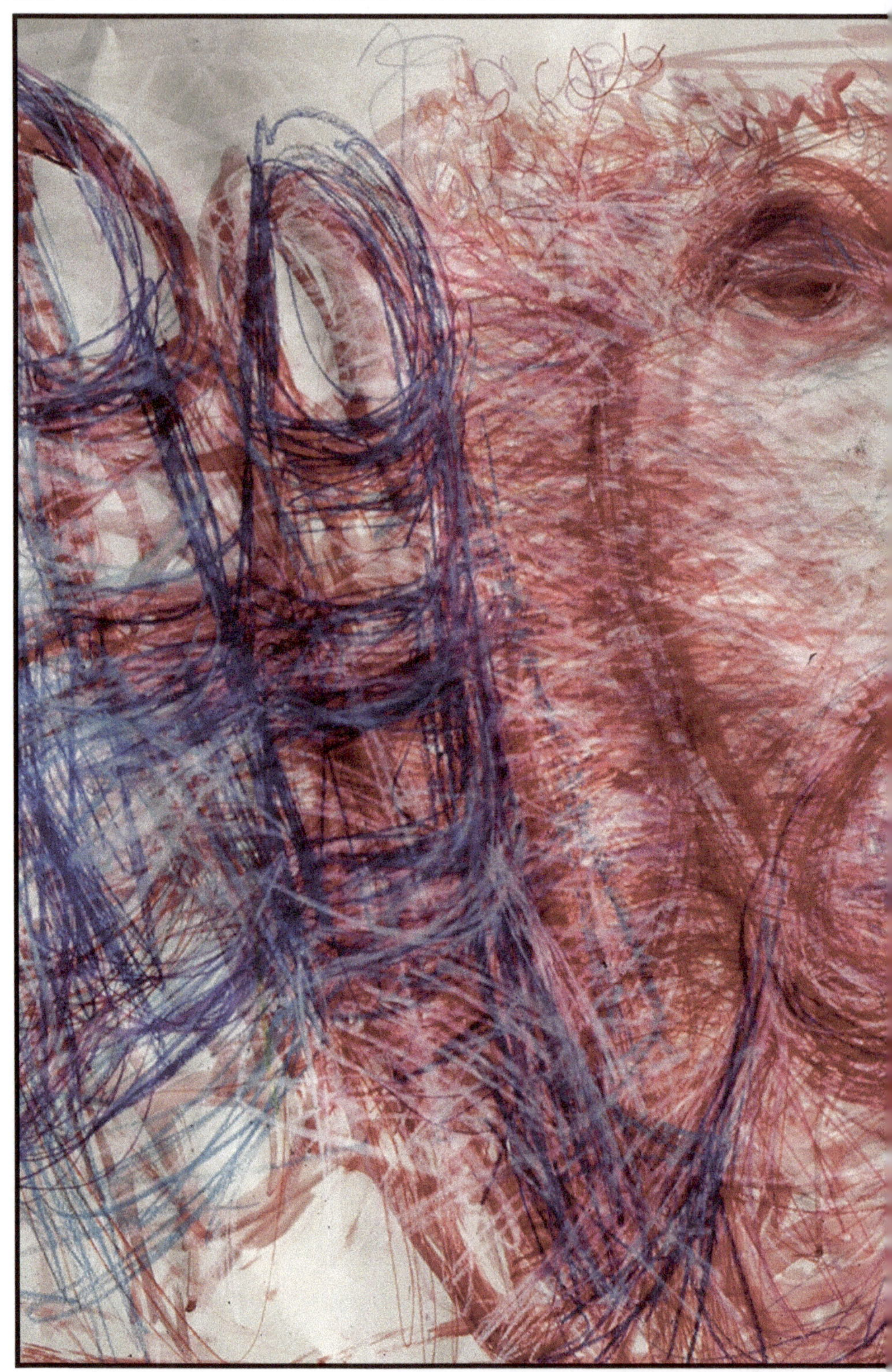

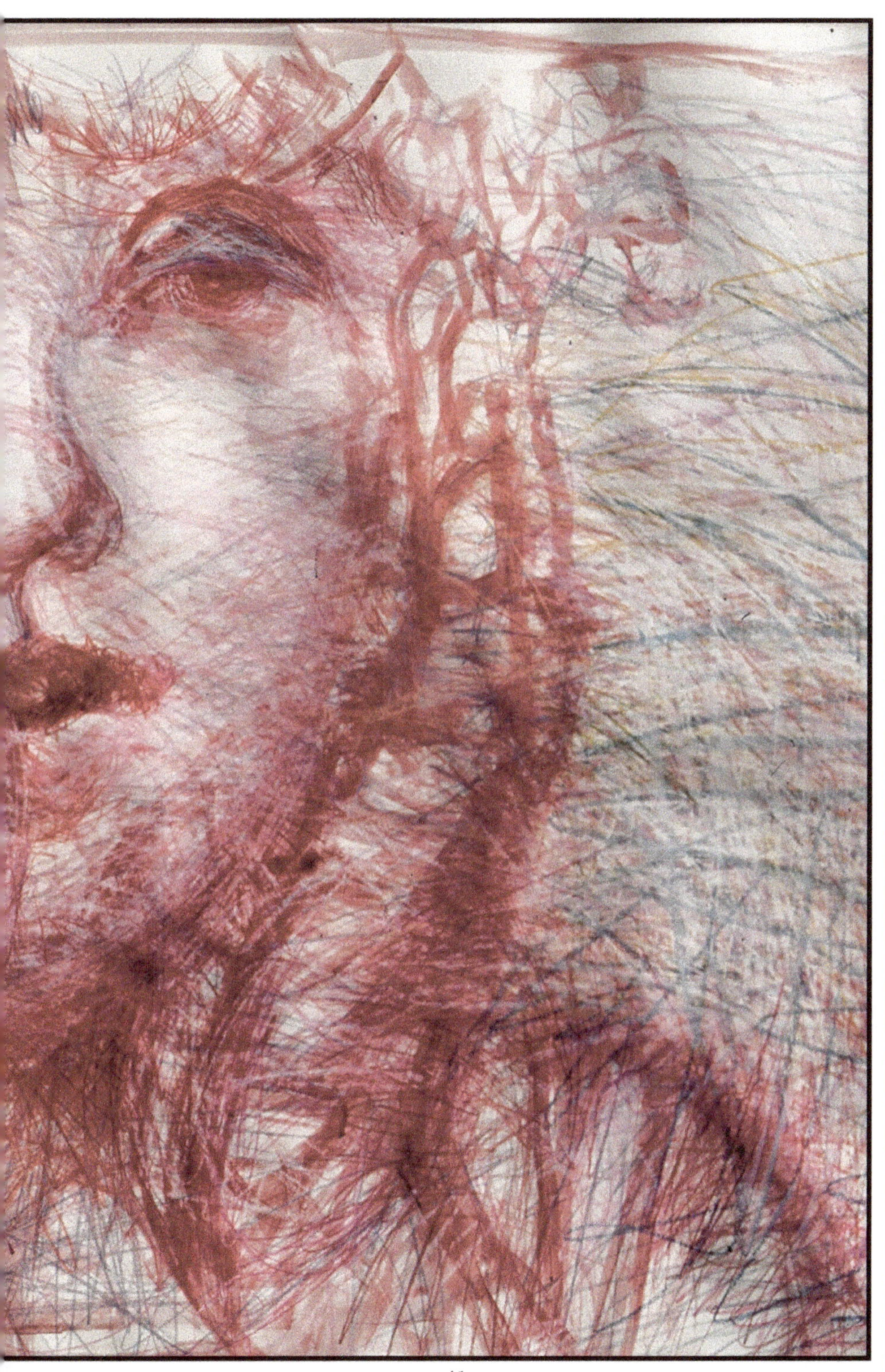

Animals under the Sun

Anthony J. Dennis

Even the pale sun in the pale sky cannot
tell of its whiteness, so how are
we to tell

of love or beauty or truth
or how the inside of an animal's cage
always looks filthy to everyone
except the animal?

Prowling, preening, positioning
ourselves under artificial incandescent suns,
housed in towers of steel and concrete.
Seeking to pounce on our peers,
take down our betters,
who are we to talk about cages
of steel and concrete?

Can the creature unlatch itself? Use the imagination
to unspool a landscape of tundra or savannah as it paces its cage?

My Struggle

Andrea Lee Dunn

The dog snores perpendicular at my feet.
I'm imprisoned by bedsheets.
The empty lilac scratches my window.
I worry its lack of blooms.
I worry the meager bees once it does.
I hear ice cubes drop into your glass
across the house. Another drink.
I worry your health. And my health.
And my sanity. Turn the white noise
up in the reaches of the night where

thoughts strangle out sleep.
Every shadow announces
the usurping of the sun.
It's over. It's over; I know
they'll grow up to be lonely
or addicts or blaming me
for thinking of dancing with
a flame that would burn everything just
so I could loosen my grip or
burrow in, or at some stabbed interval

just let the lid off and finally
cry. I'd be a volcano—
a wake of molten rock running
down hot cheeks, wasting everything
for a moment of relief from turning
over and over until the thoughts
are so threadbare
they can't even be held. But then,
a sapling is just a burned pinecone,
scales pinned by a recollection in

daylight, finally come, pressed through the
darkest hour to daybreak.

At first light my lungs birth repent
and remorse, prayers for another round
of forgiveness and grace
and dewdrops and fresh things
of the waking world, risen once again
from the shallow grave. Oh hands, oh
children, oh husband, oh fragile me,
a better self begs its hands out to you.

Kids Don't Sound That Great To Me

Grace Dilger

2.

My wouldn't-be ancestral home may be a portal,
that's what the Psychic with the taffy lipstick
stuck on her incisor is saying. Specifically,
she thinks the painting in my cousin's bedroom
of the woman who looks like she's just seen
what this Psychic charges, could be a portal
beyond the veil or whatever. My mother first
wondered what a woman would taste like here,
maybe. More boringly she took her first steps,
her raccoon tore up the Christmas presents,
she broke her first bone, she ate, like thirty different
turkeys here. I hunted for Easter eggs under flint
puffs of my father's cigarettes, once, here. Most years
the smoke was my Aunt's, who had her last
conscious thought, in her sweatpants, on the red
and white oak of the kitchen floor, here.

When I was softer and smaller this was the mashed
potatoes house. Safe and filling. Now it's not unlike
my city's subway in this unprecedented mental health
cataclysm. You swerve to avoid humans in crisis, you hop
over their literal shit, turn away from their indignity,
steady yourself for the amount of penises you're
guaranteed to see this week. Sometimes you bring
extra muffins to give them because you fancy yourself
a Nice White Lady but mostly you don't call your Senator
and mostly your muffins ain't shit. Trauma bombs, that's
what I'm avoiding in my wouldn't-be ancestral home.
This place is all wet walnuts and butter bells, the charming
Febrezes of yesteryear. There's a glaze of grime
the way we pretend that's all the Trump years were.
Yes, there would be toilet paper, and hand-soap,
and clean tub-caulking for grandbabies if some of us hadn't died,
but we did, so now we can pretend that actually that was it,
and that's why Charlene is now asking if she can touch
my breast bone to better connect with my life-force.

I always thought I'd nestle mulberry and periwinkle eggs under
sprinkler systems and mosaic frogs in the yard for my babies

here. I'd mash like my mother had mashed like her mother before
her, the potatoes on the GE electric stovetop. The bang would be
the bang of my love, the stream of milk, 2%, my devotion to even
their bones. The bronze bottle opener, the galvanized bread box,
for God's sake, the poppy-printed linen napkins —no more
emblems of their era than Job's fucking Apple is now. Our time is
deforested, asphalted, shock-blanket-silver. The peach pinkies
of toddlers wrapped around kennels, the woodbury-ivory Cole Haans
of free murderers on marble court steps, the glint of their badges, the grins
of their wives. To tell my child the world is his would be to confirm
his supremacy. Charlene here tells me I'll have three.

1.

My mother's love language is laundry, balled socks and spot-treated blouses.
Her mother's love language was laundry too, by the cargo ship load.
I used to think it was her favorite thing, to wash what her family had sullied.
In the 60s, Grandma owned a cat called Tippy who used to piss in the toaster.
Burnt by her husband, schmeared with domesticity which crusted her genius,
Grandma presented the rancid Wonder Bread with margarine to her five
children.
Apparently, this feline behavior is indicative of major kidney infection.
Tippy associated his litter box with pain. But Grandma couldn't stomach
litter boxes, wouldn't keep them in the house. The cats relieved themselves
in the yard, on the summer lilac, the tulips, and especially, the dogwood.
My mother, her sisters and her brother knew better than to insult their moth-
er.
Emptiness was not an option. My mother still winces at kittens and cringes
at convection ovens, is still thinking of the buttery, pickle and piss on white
bread,
of the mushroom cloud over her tongue, Munch's Scream inside her head.
Tippy's two acres of pain. And just when she'd gotten used to it,
thought it had passed, on the roof of her mouth—
the sticky ttt-tt, of her mother's broken heart.

L A G T I M E

Kimberly Kradel

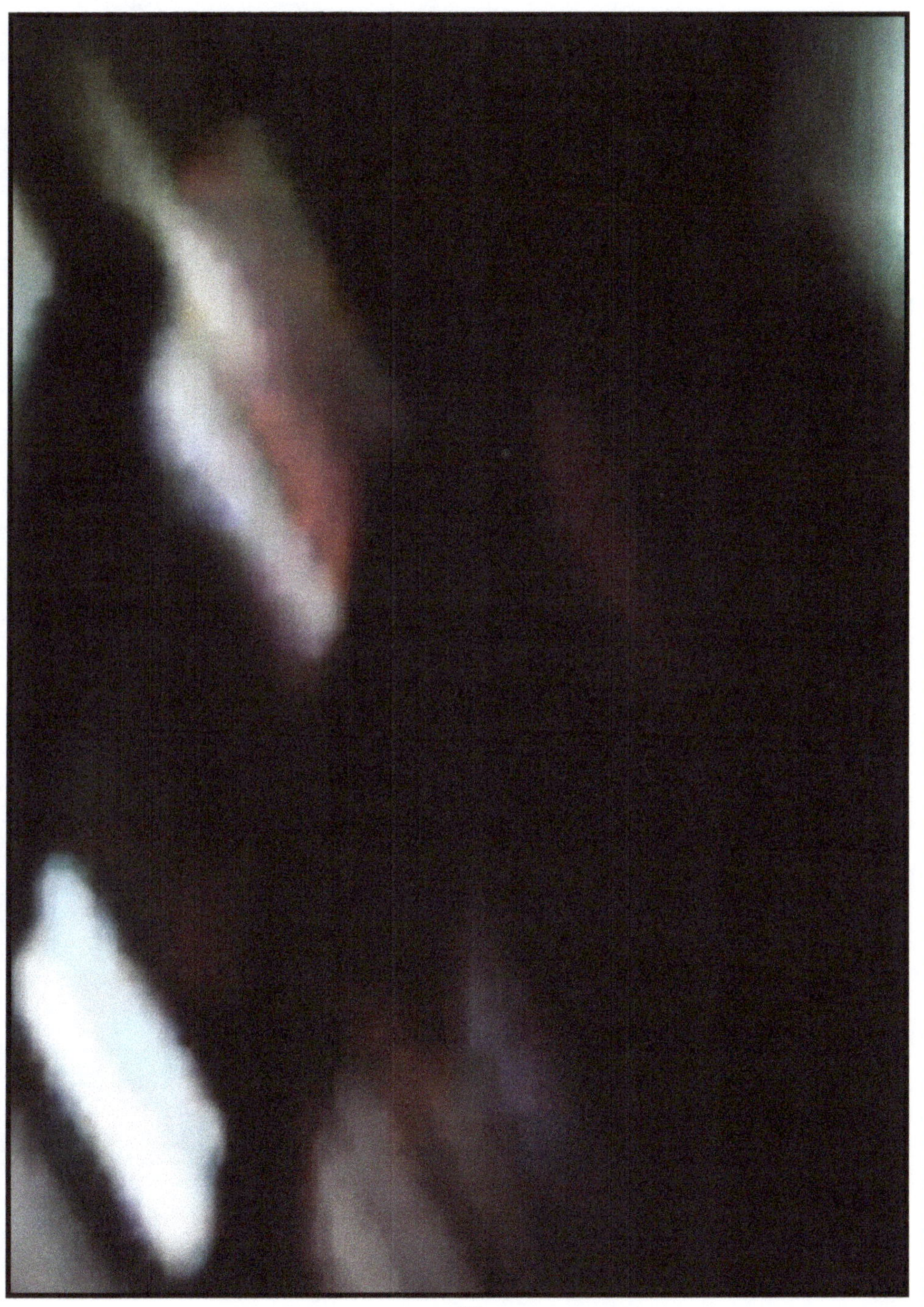

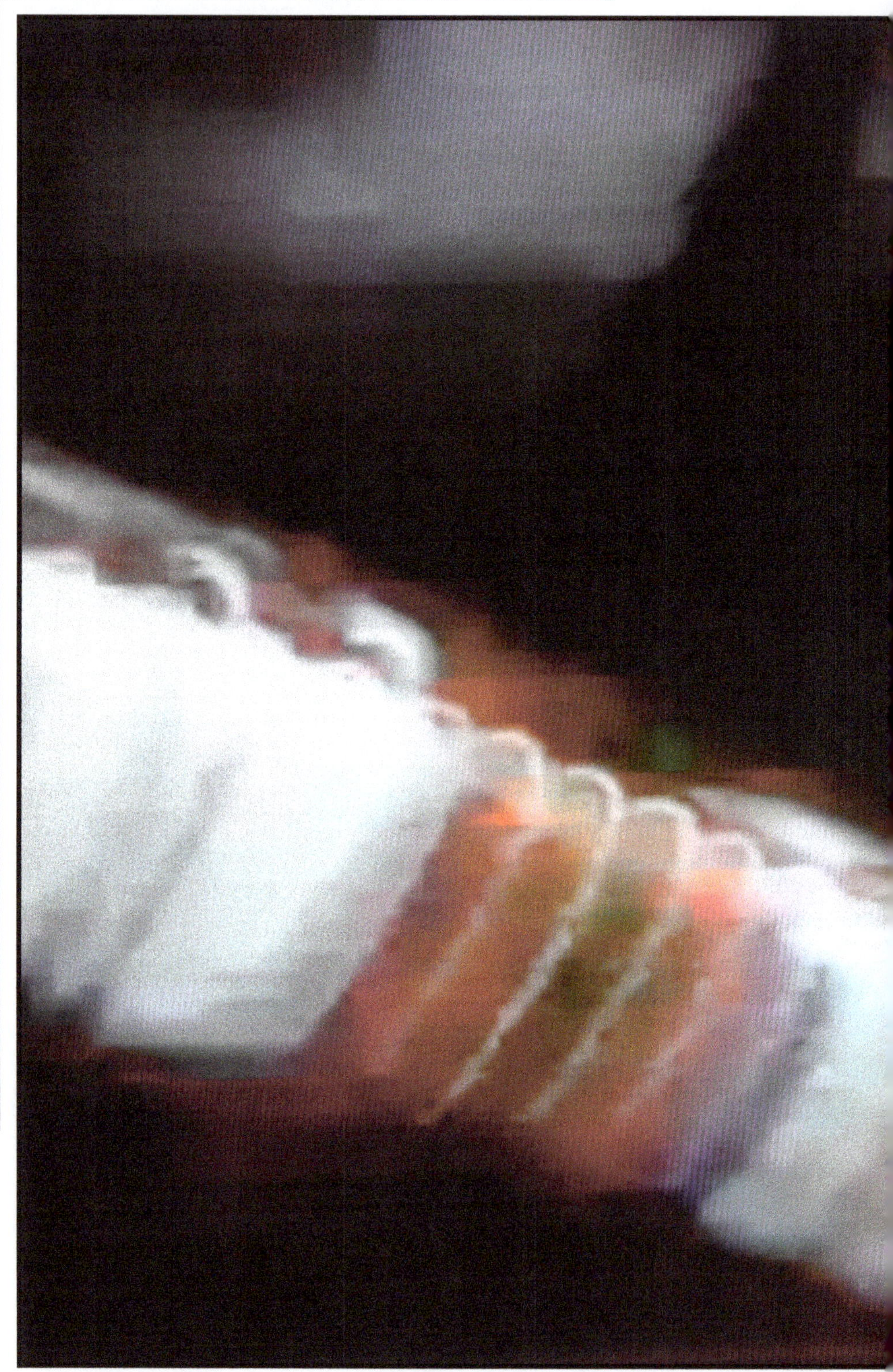

The Nitrous Dealer's Beautiful Wife

Christopher Norcross

Falls into herself
Through the grime on the windowpane,

Where arpeggios of water
Form on the ceiling and coalesce.

Ripples, Pulled by the droop of the hour.
Bent toward the cover of a nocturnal world,

By nape of the neck,
Or thin, clammy palm on the plexiglass divider.

Between waking worlds,
Seasick through expectation,

At the metropolitan mausoleum,
Where they work over the displays like matisse on high stilts,

A clerical quiet comes suddenly untangled,
The knot of confusion breaks,

She dithers,
And through the maze of lithe bodies,
Follows a mark with a limp, indifferent eye,
Runs all along them
In circles,
Down stairways,

Breathing truth into hard truth
Into hardly hearing ears,

Where the people blush with poppies,
Idling in the glow of a rented hour
And a god's eye view of an apocalyptic ocean.

Seeing the night in daylight detail,
With no way to tell it.

Folie A Deux

Mac Chandler

they say the farmer
that birthed the thing
afterward ate every
glass window in his house,
swigged down the
entire lake of his backyard
in one wet gulp.

the two-headed lamb
stares away from itself,
avoids window gazing
like cholera.
a creature doubled over
its first day of life,
an evolutionary miracle of
american horror.

after all the hem and haw,
when the farmer met
his own eyes anyway
on the shine of his trusty axe,
he killed the little beast
as easy as blowing heads from
a twin of daisies to make two
wishes at once, then buried
it's severed self
in the dirt in the night
with two gravestones.

Florence in Motion

John Lightle

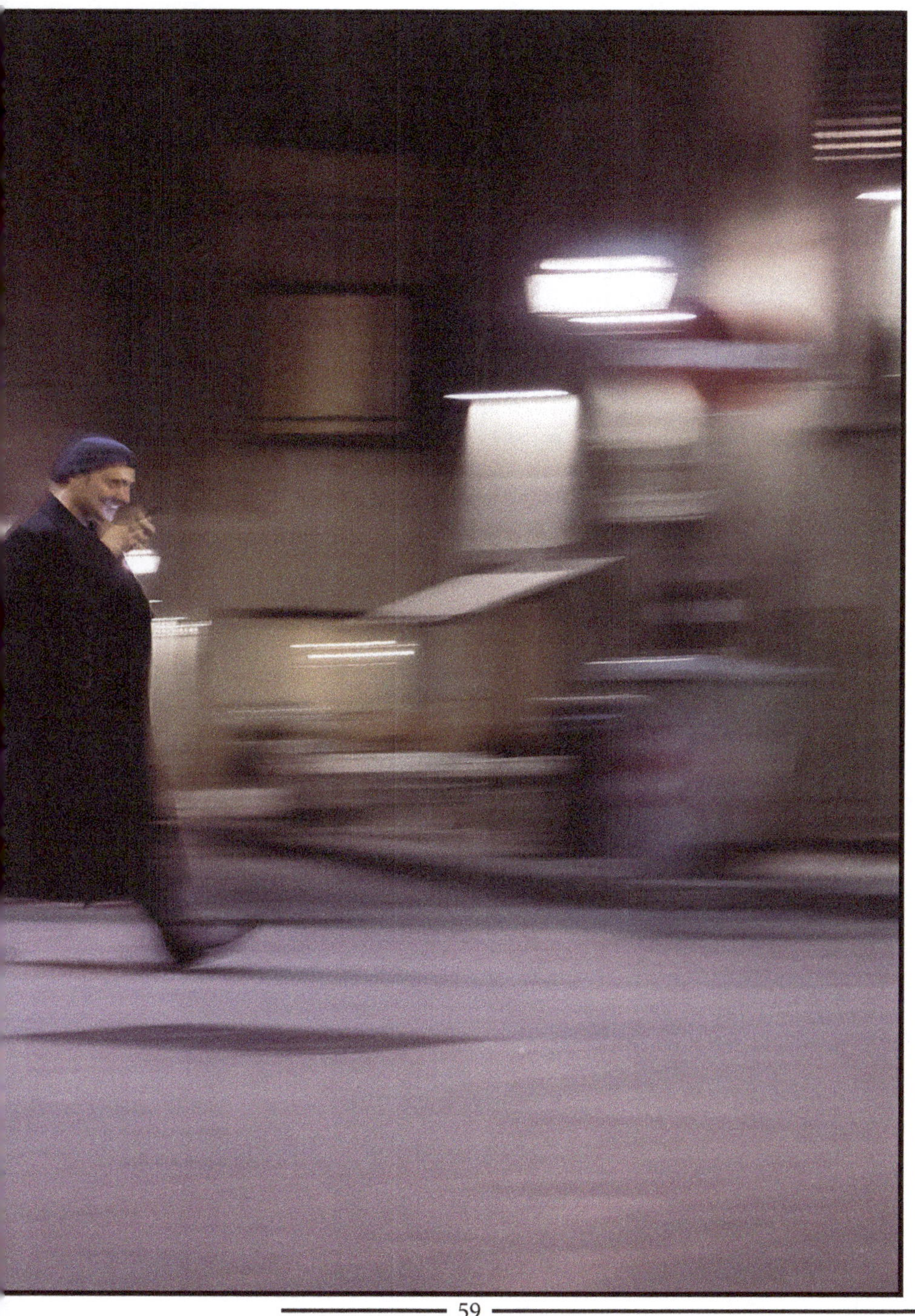

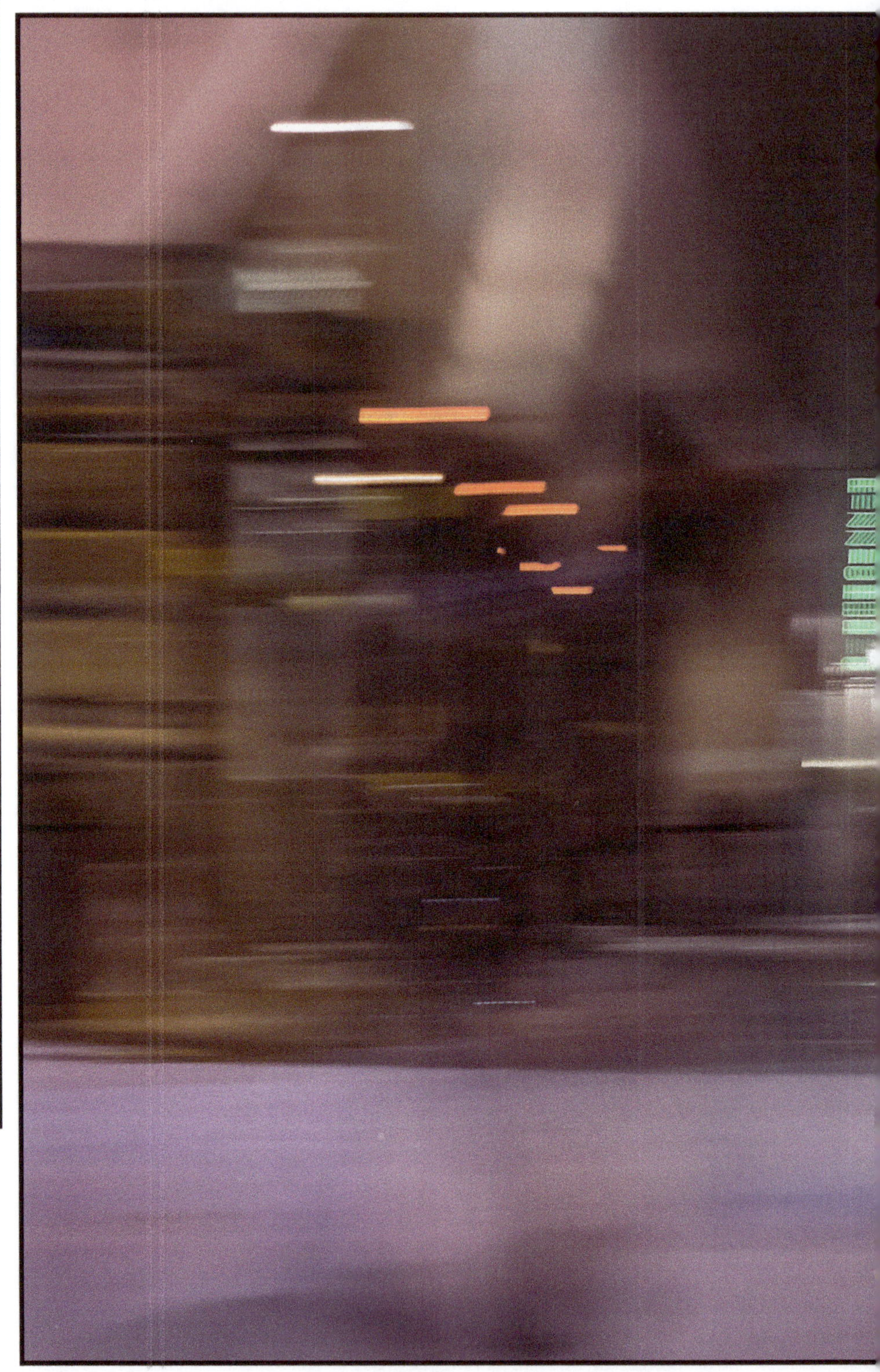

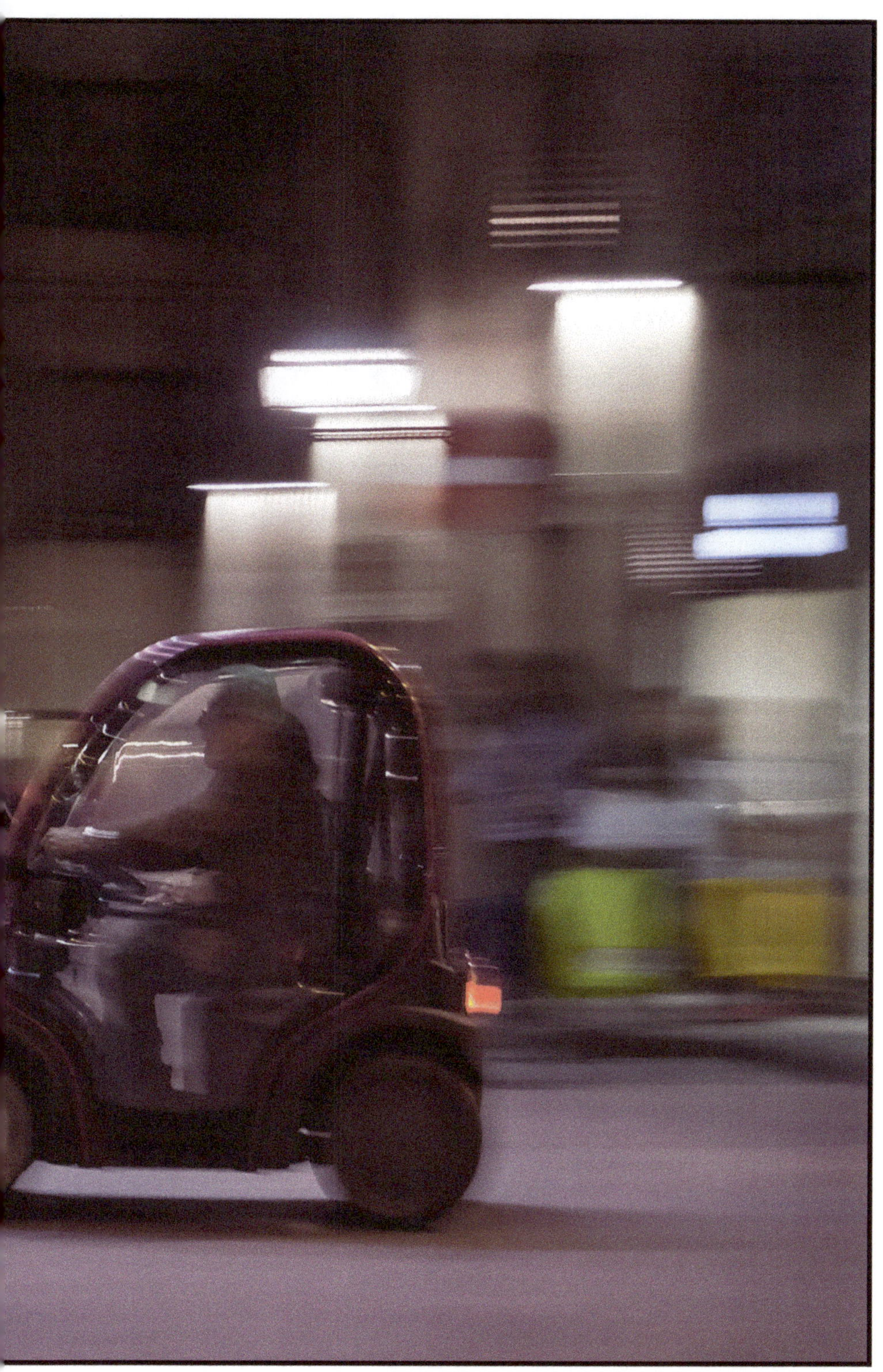

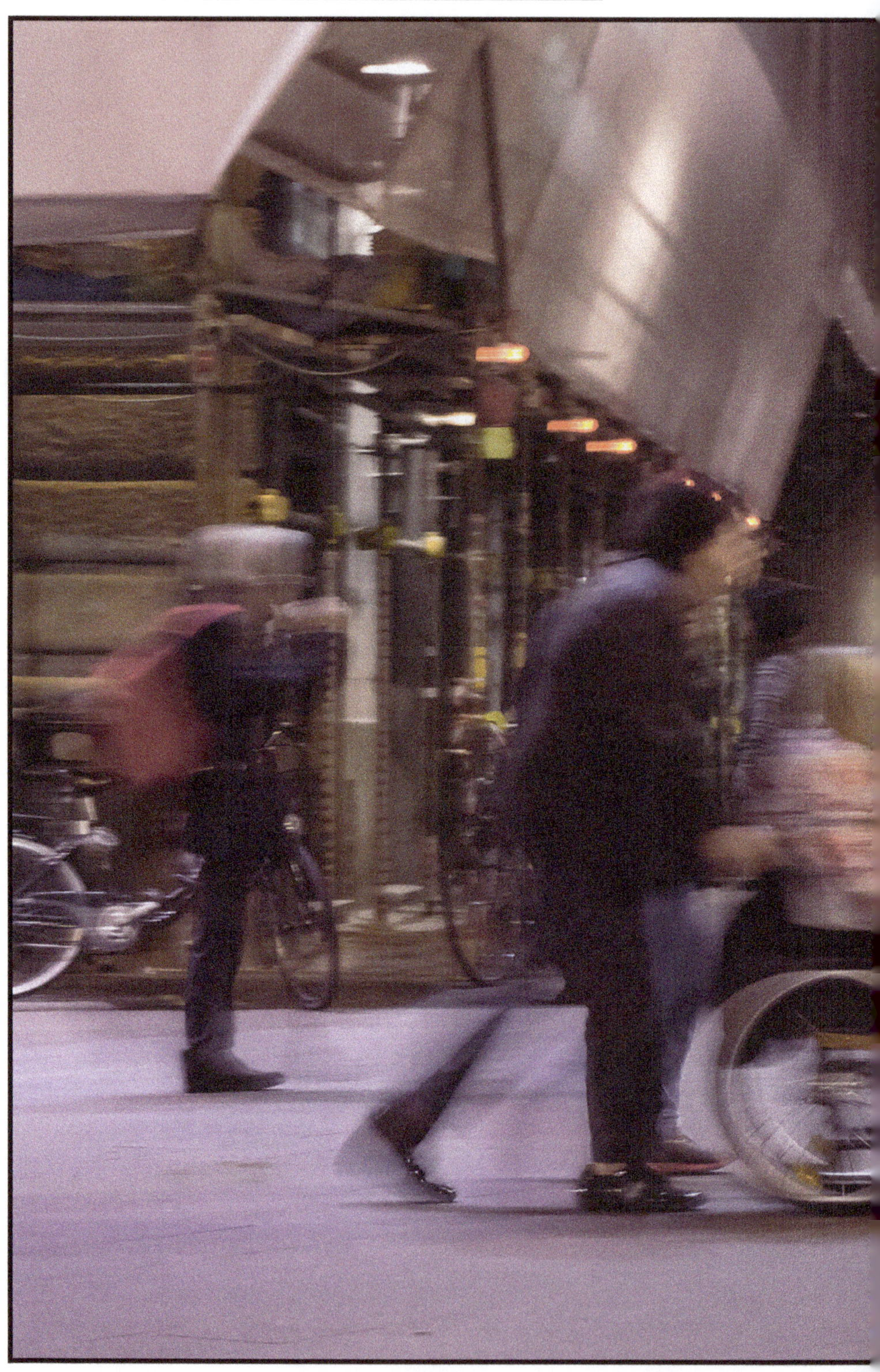

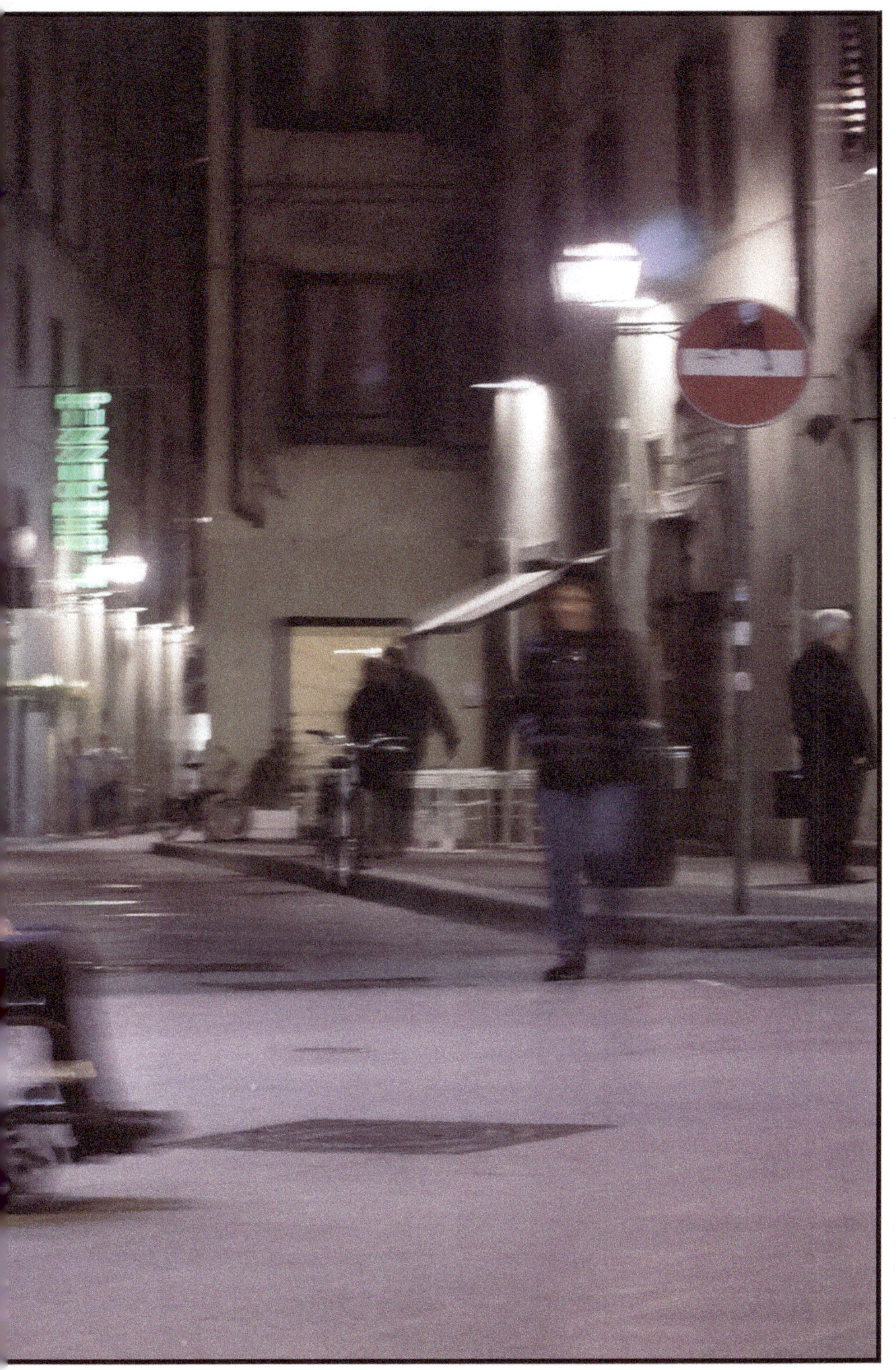

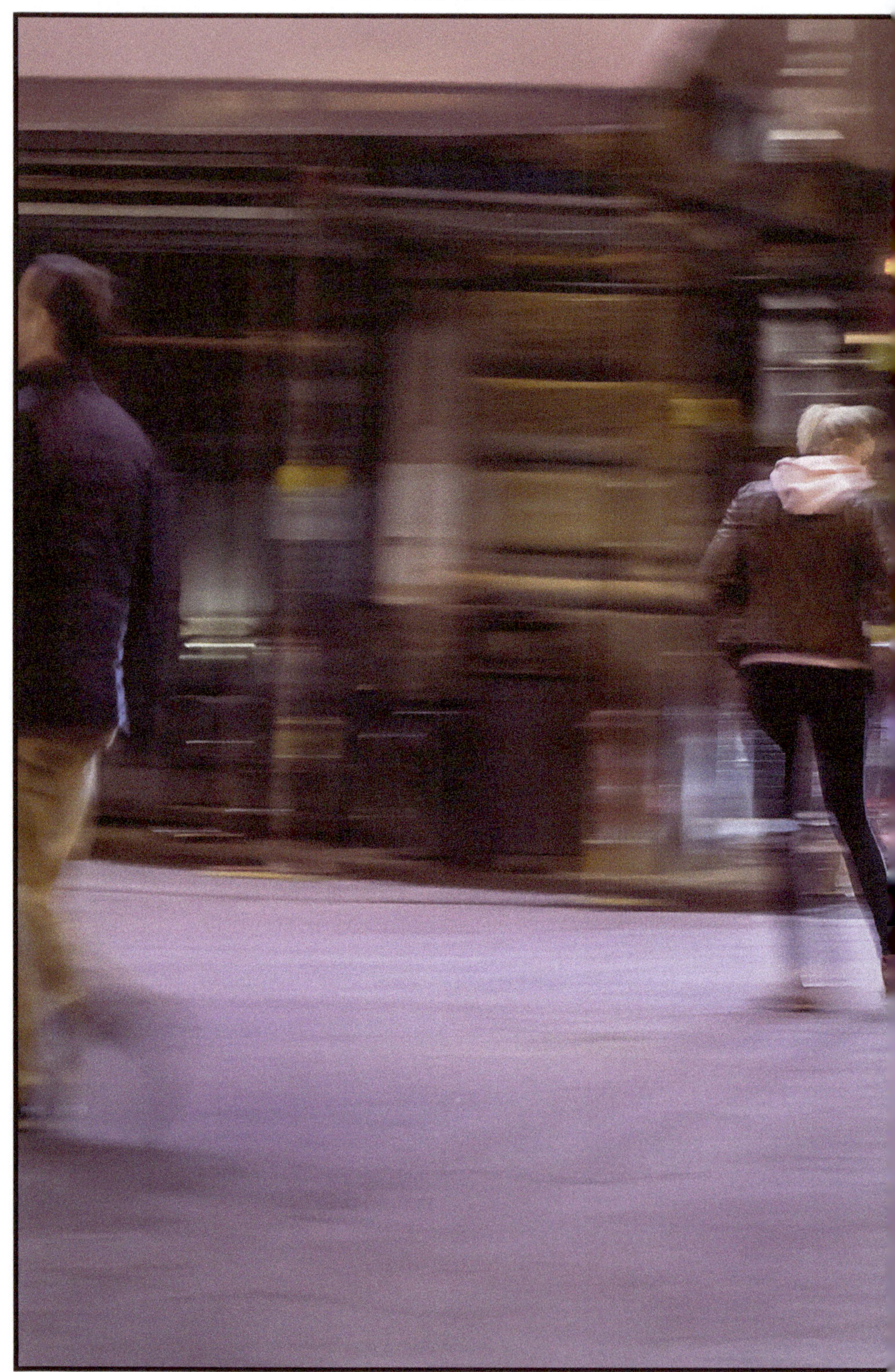

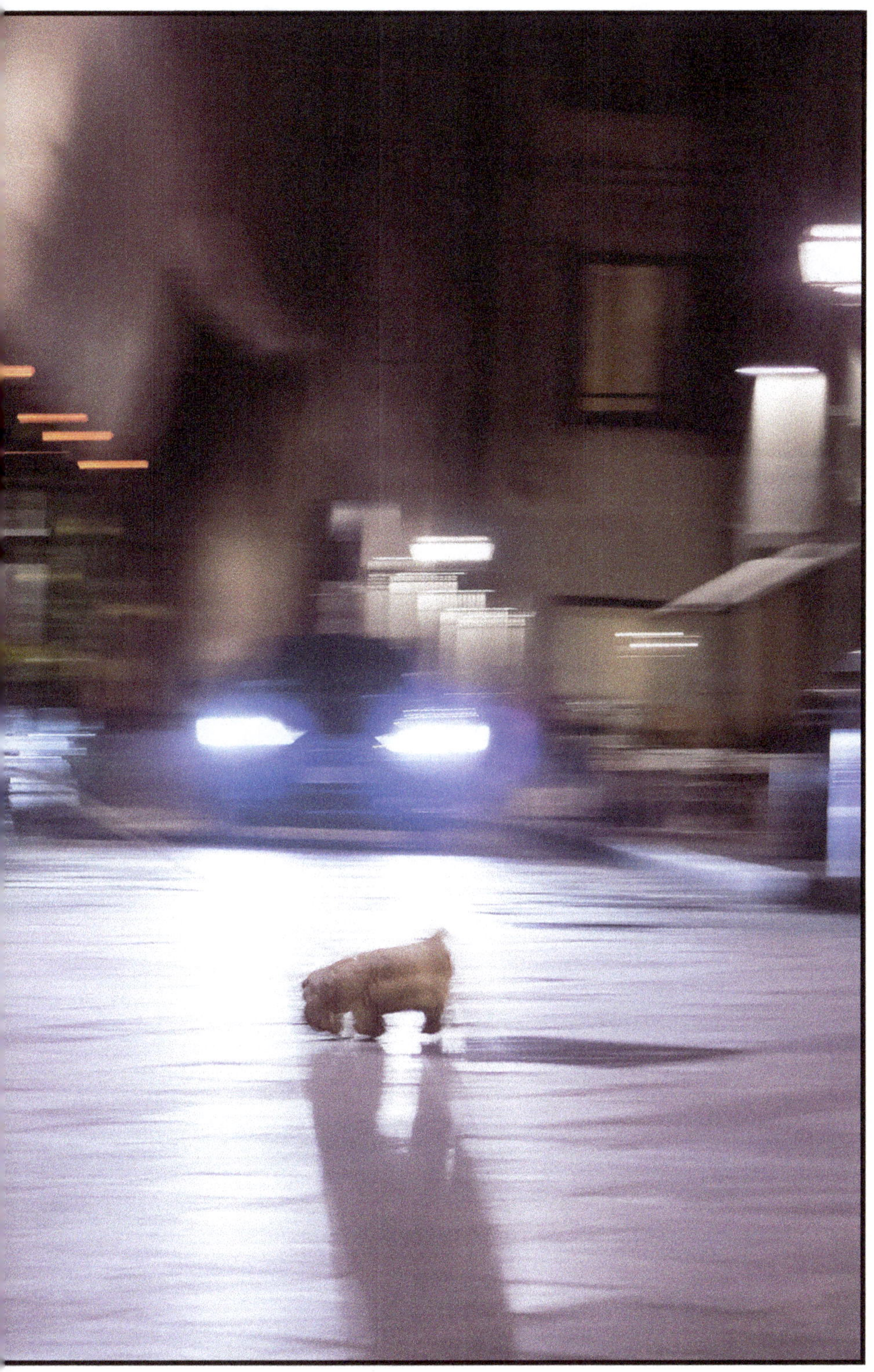

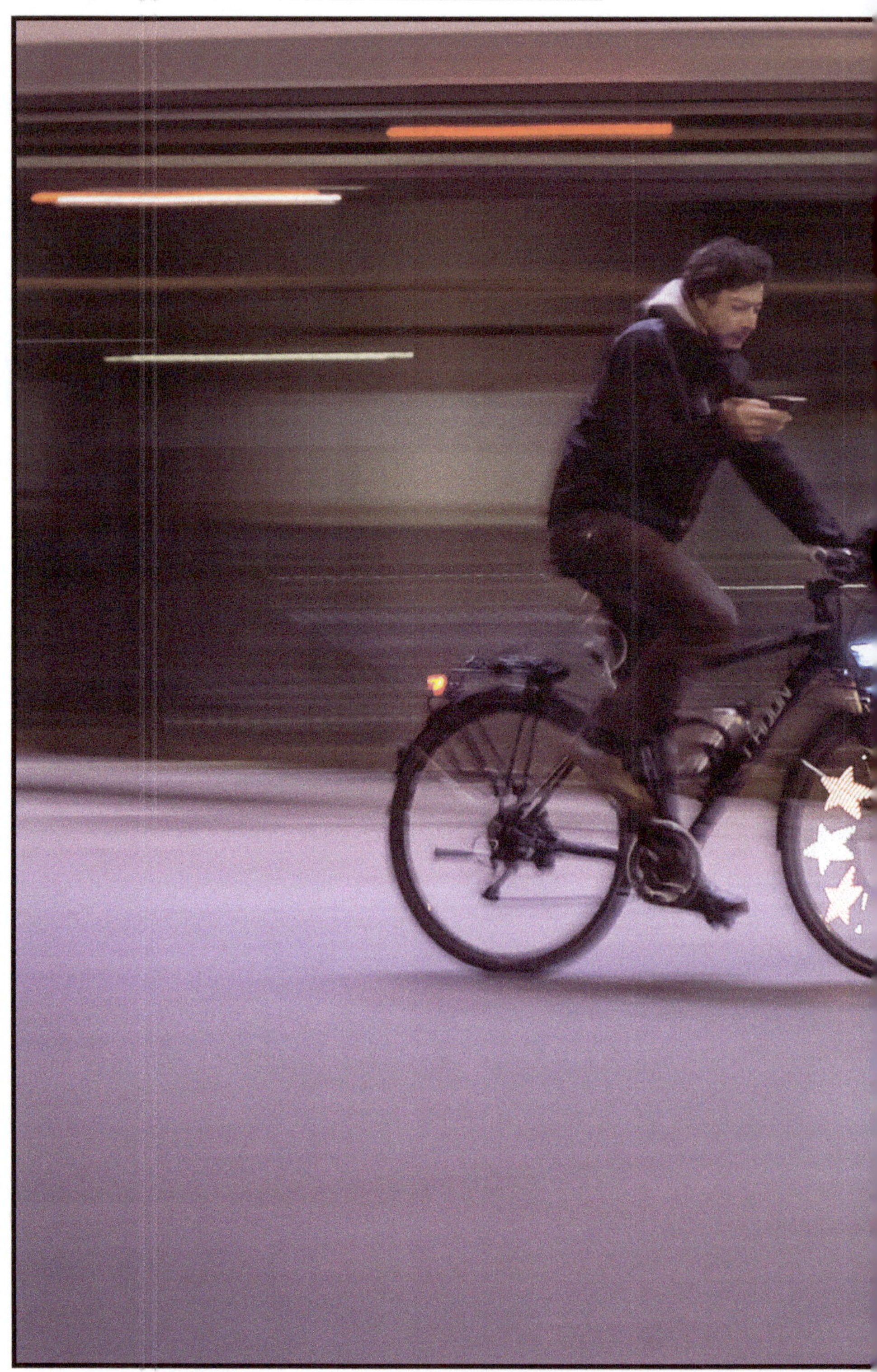

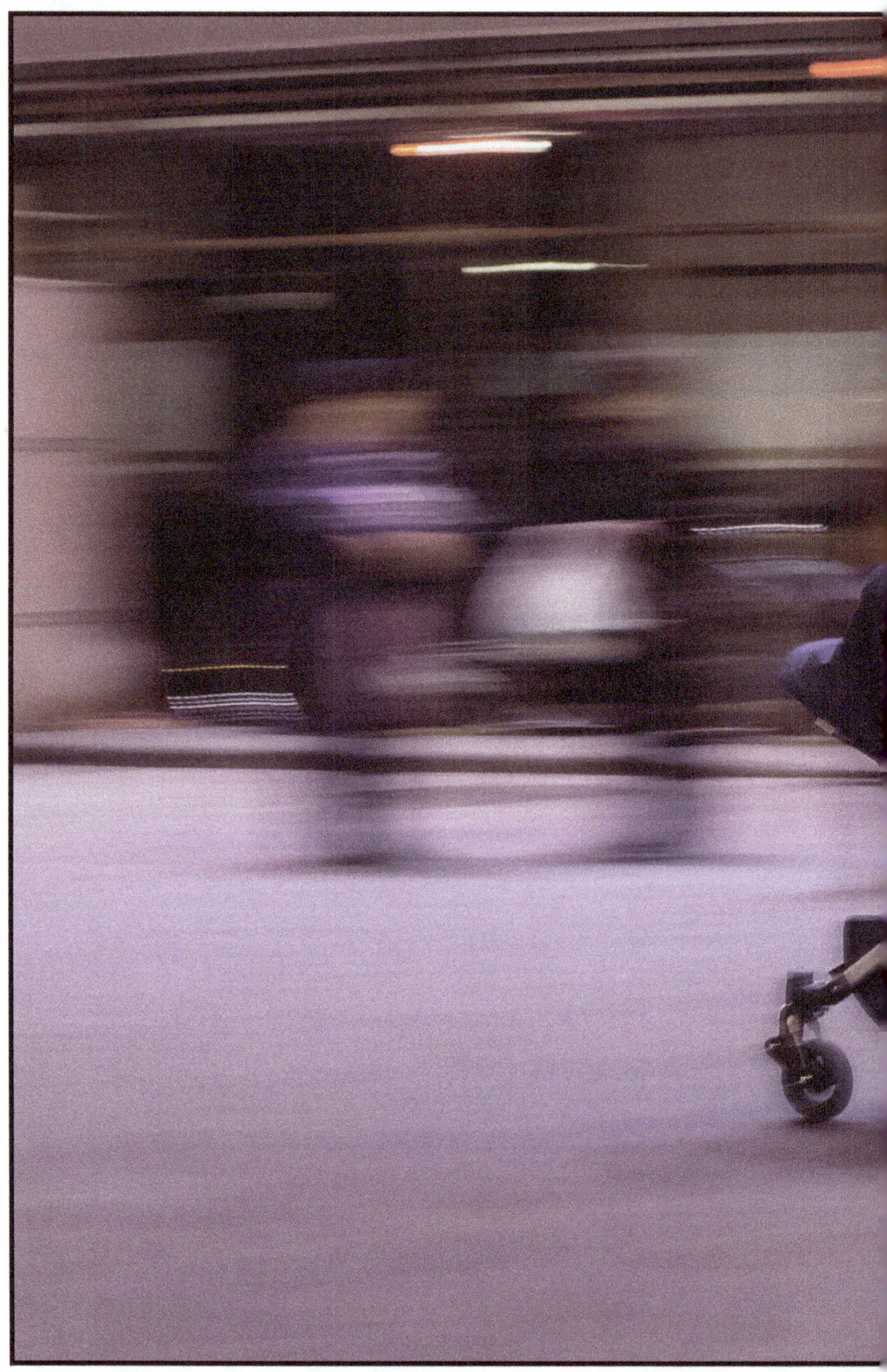

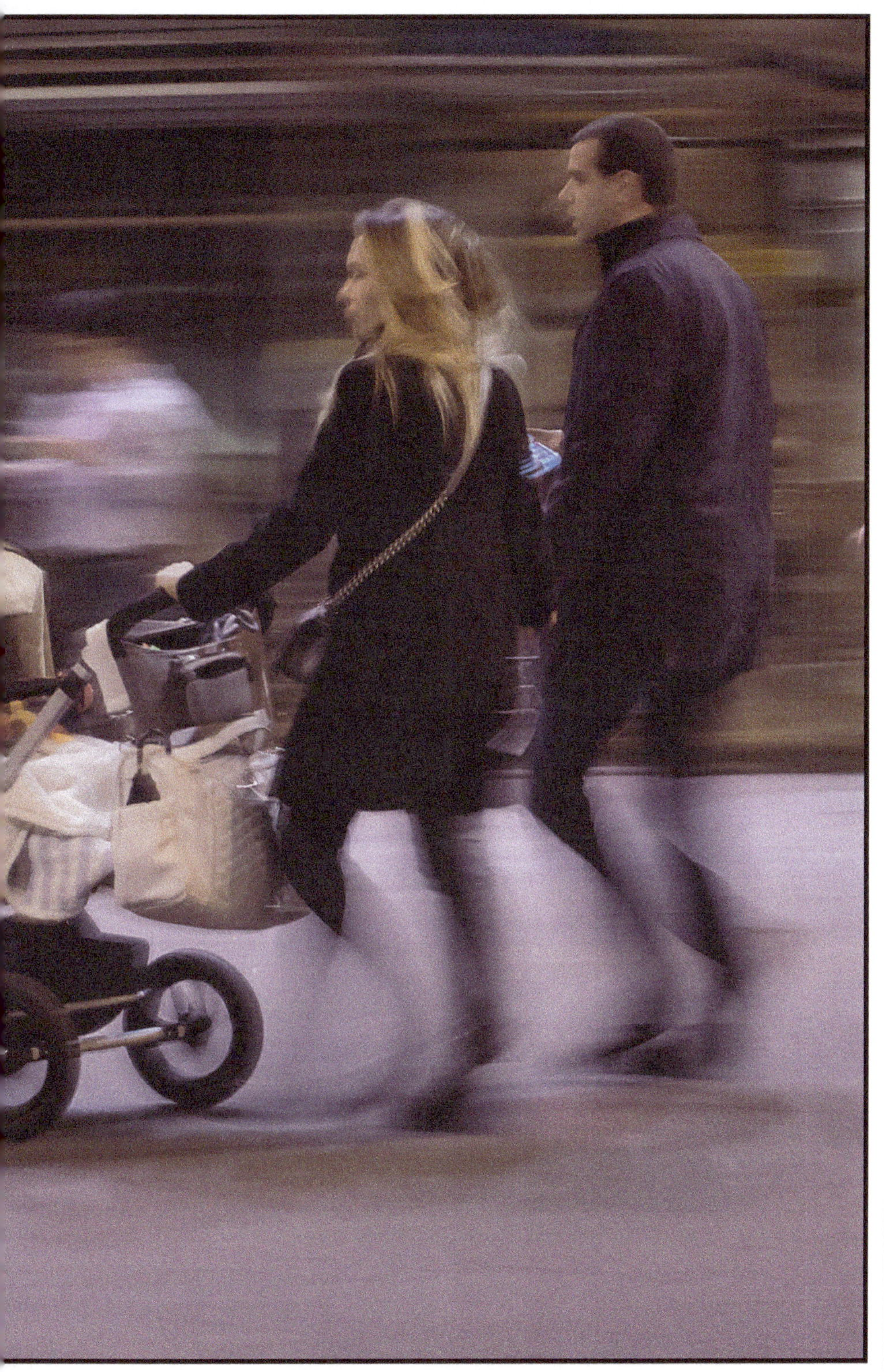

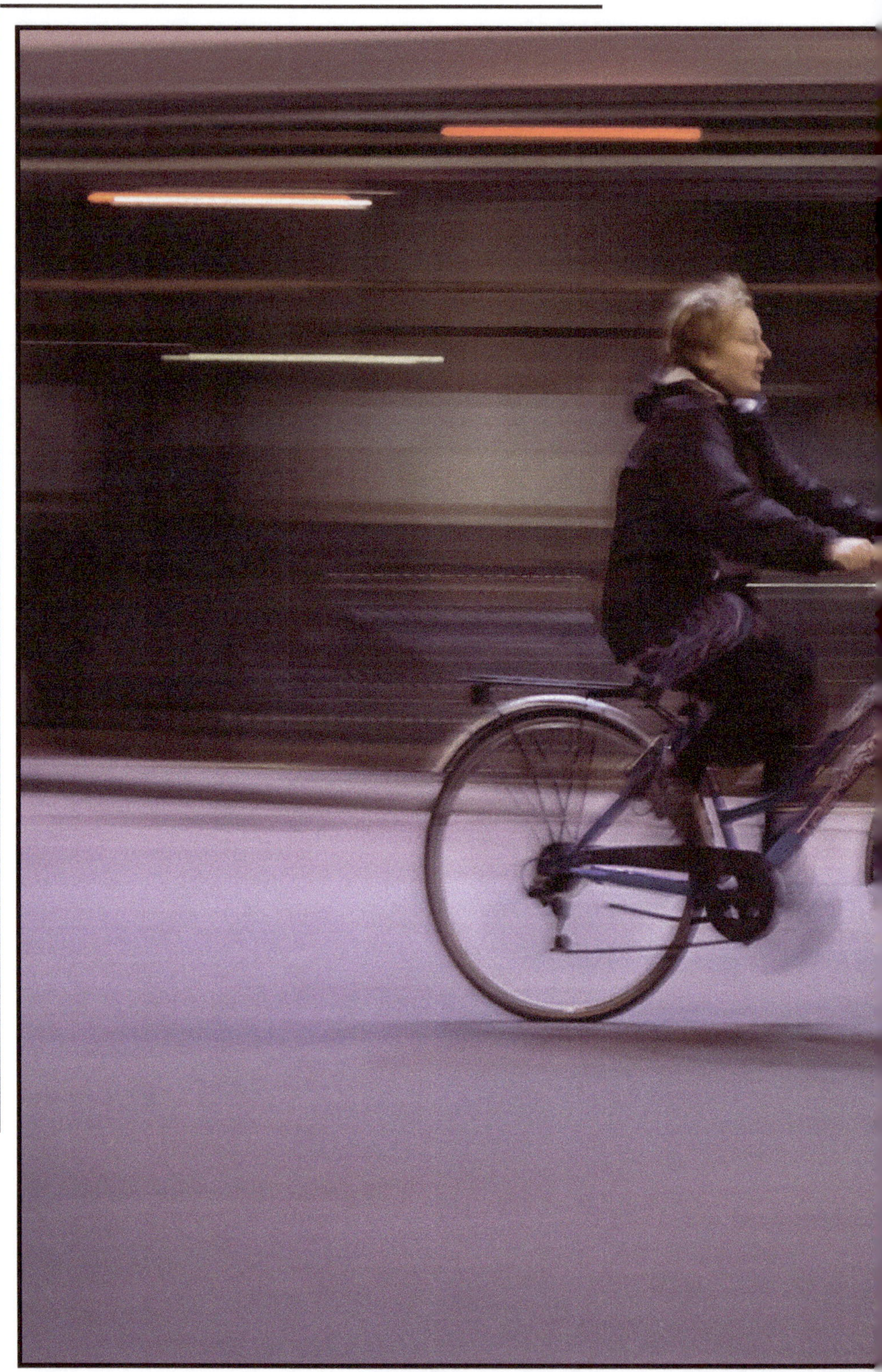

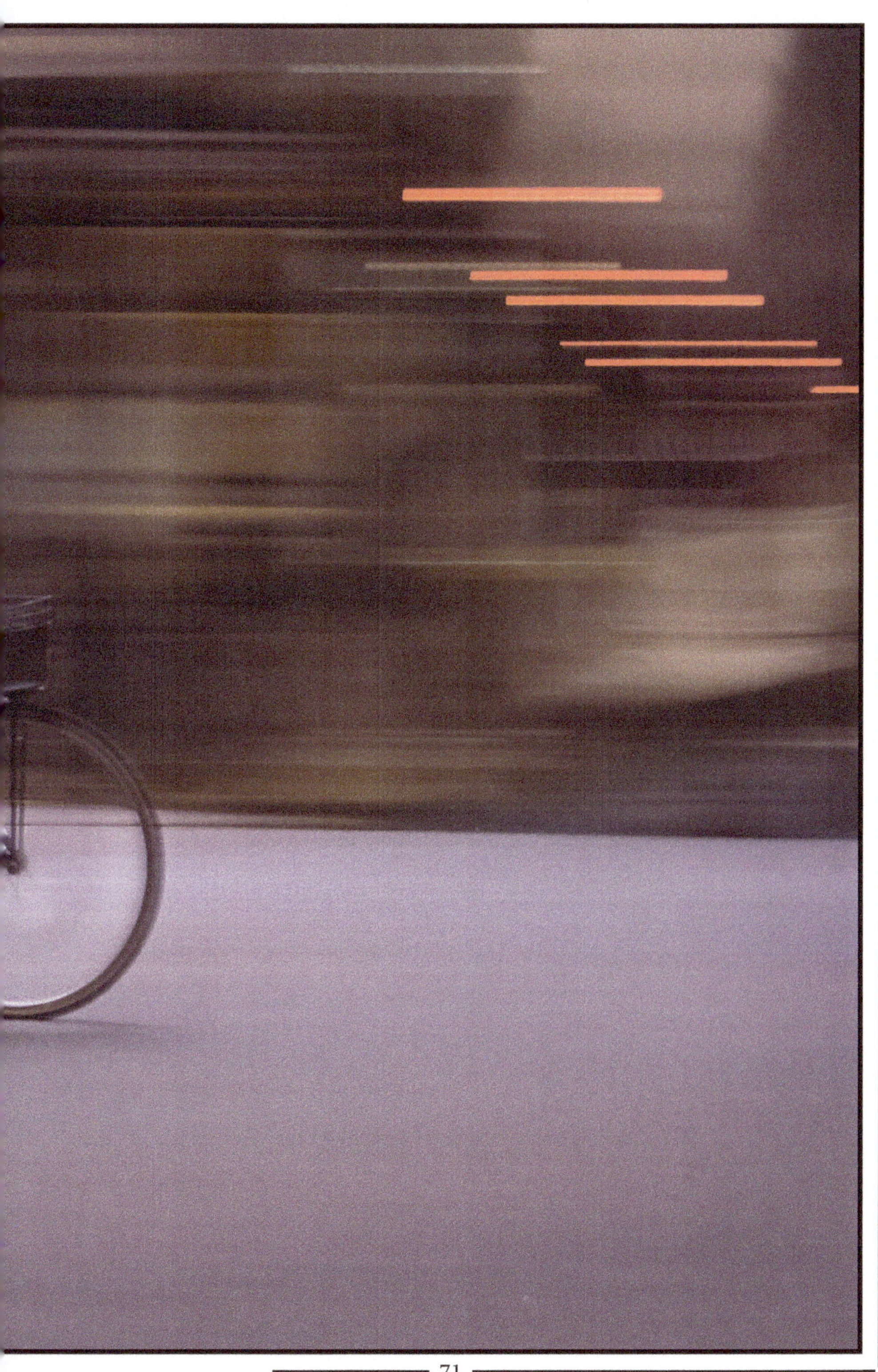

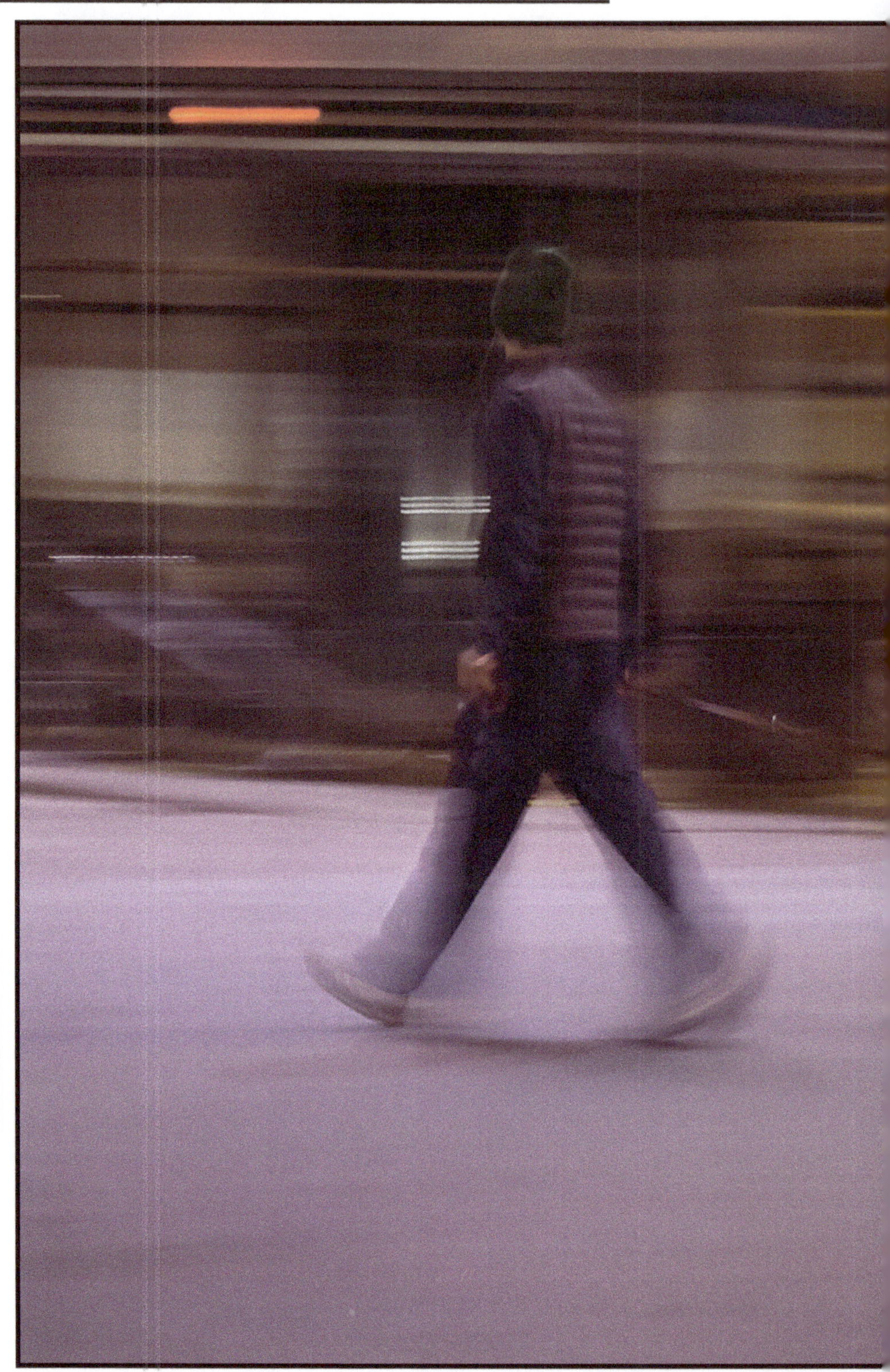

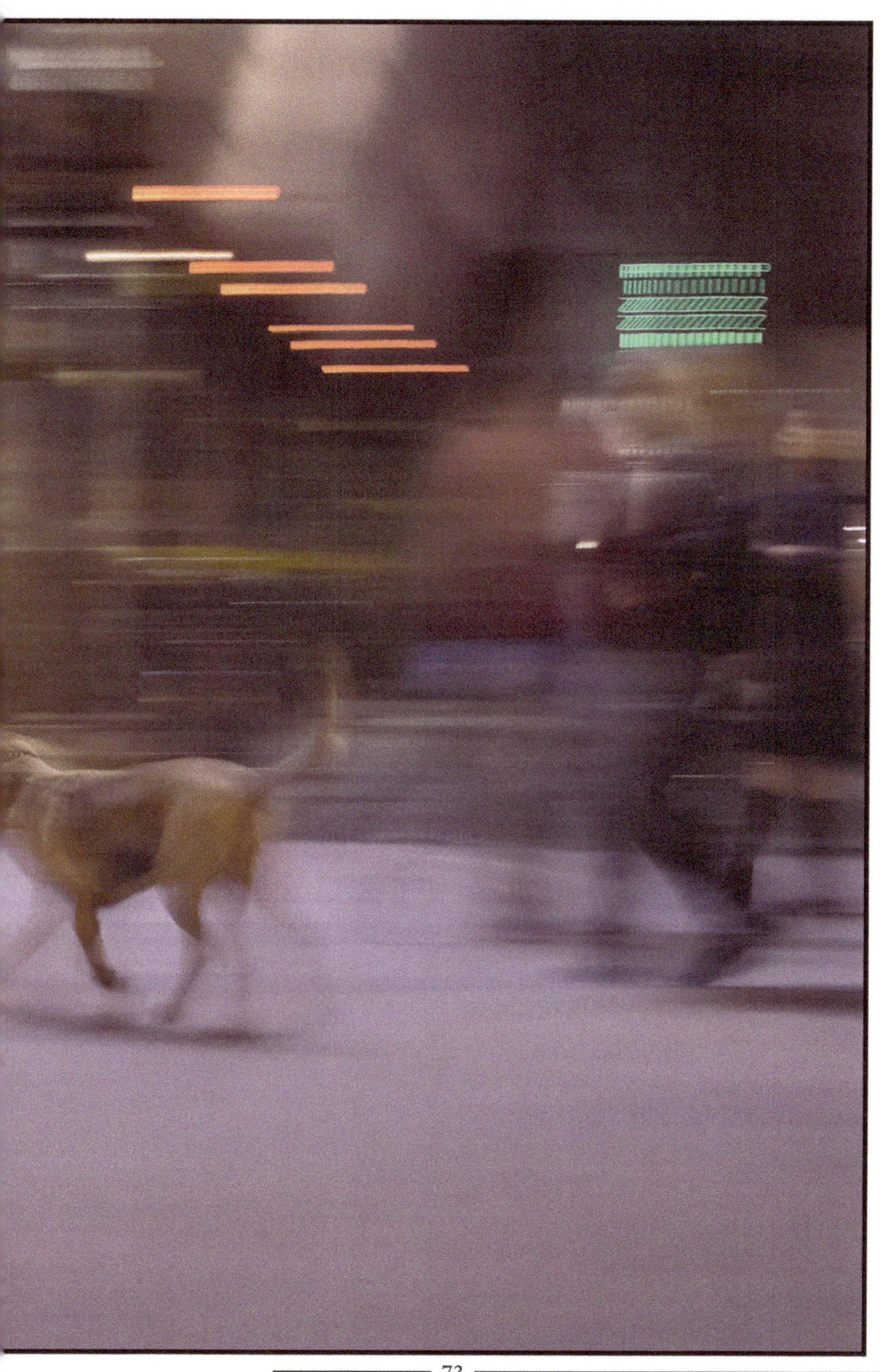

Citrus and Asbestos: The Tale of Amos

Sam Waldron

Amos in tan-white shawl, splotched with fruit stains,
crossed the Nullarbor leaving in his wake a trail of syrup.

He traded his remaining figs and grapes for a brass trumpet;
tried three notes, then four, until the trumpet squeaked a dry blast.

The blast reached fat owners in stone houses,
cracks rippled through their ceilings –
they held a meeting –
electing the same solution that they tried for calamities three and four:
raise taxes on straw.

Amos gave to the farmers pairs of oars
and set their horses to ploughing the oceans.
On the shores the rich were wailing,
as the poor harvested ambergris, sailing
sweet scents through low plains, singing
wet songs from fertile lungs.

Stones fell through ivory-adorned ceilings and poison
infected poisoned justice – court adjourned.
Out of the stench the lords and ladies went to their
Summer houses to find nothing but lemon stains.
Winter houses to find nothing but lime stains.
Riding the risings and fallings of autumn and spring
with neither saddle or stirrup.

I went to the seaside and Amos told me that sheep spit
Makes ideal trumpet lubricant. I gave him my thanks, and made my escape.

I went to the orchard and Amos told me that the laws of physics

helped him recover from insomnia. I gave him my thanks,
and made my escape.

I went to the sunken city and Amos told me that
the higher the suspension point of the plum line,
the more accurate the measurement. I gave him my thanks,
dried my hands, and made my escape.

Back above the surface the lords and ladies
had resorted to living in baskets, far from their
apple-crumbled past. Having given up pursuit of property,
they settled for purchasing the poor,
only to push them out into pilfered paddocks.

Blotched Amos brought to the slaves a basket of ripe fruit.
Drooling and dripping met in mouths,
and seeds sprang up in stomachs
watered by wet lungs
until they flourished in the fervent hands,

that will forever make gardens and eat their fruit.

The Agent's Critique

N.M. Campbell

MSD Literary Agency
1 Grand Army Plaza,
Brooklyn, NY 11238
February 28, 2016

Anonymous
PO Box 1836 – Cooper Union
New York, New York 10003
Re: 24 Hour Response and Critique

To Whom? It May Concern:

A literary agent sifts through piles of dreams. The best way to avoid the hard-to-edit authors is by finding holes in the story. There are many in your manuscript. Further complicating your package is that there are multiple versions of the same text. Some appear to be drafts and others are in multiple languages, some more ancient than modern. Furthermore, these revisions are joined to layers of analysis in addition to official acclamation.

The work is already published, but as you indicated in your cover letter, readership is more and more limited. You are seeking clarification about what might be keeping this text out of newer generations' hands. The amici curiae writing on your behalf, however, suggest there is something universal about this text and it merits continued publication. Therefore, I read beyond the first five pages of your sample chapter "Genesis."

The lack of representation from half of the population is as frustrating as a missing puzzle piece. Female character development is minimal. In "Genesis," women are only named to distinguish between polyamorous wives who give birth to important men. One such nameless woman stands out—literally. Lot's wife becomes a pillar of salt having looked back at wicked Sodom. Her punishment is dehumanization by being turned into an inanimate object. Because of the supplementary notes provided for my review, however, she has indeed been assigned a name. Edith is not just a footnote on the tourist plaque

of history; her role in the destruction of Sodom was clarified over genera-
tions.

According to rabbinical interpretations, she is even given dialogue.
She chides her husband by comparing him to Abraham, whom she decries
as fanatical. Then she alerts Sodom to the presence of newcomers by re-
questing an excessive amount of salt from her neighbors. This action alerts
the town to unknown outsiders in their midst. Sodomites liked to know
everyone quite personally. Therefore, Lot is absolved from the responsibili-
ty of being forced to offer his virgin daughters to protect his guests.

This is one such hole in the story. Why is this Lot's reaction?
Even in the world created thus far in the manuscript, this a novel idea.
His daughters, however, are rejected because the wicked neighbors are
far more interested in Lot's heavenly, masculine guests. These messen-
gers were sent to save Lot from the impending destruction of Sodom. He
escapes, loses his wife along the way, and heads to the hills with his two
daughters.

Lot's daughters wholly understand their role in sacred lineage,
back to Uncle Abraham and Adam before him. They devise a plan to get their
father drunk for the purpose of continuing this spiritual destiny. But there
is little additional analysis of their decision in your manuscript. Perhaps
this is valid: Psychological trauma can lead to action without thought, viz.,
Stockholm Syndrome.

These young women are offered for a gang rape. They flee their
home under duress. They understand the loss of their mother, though they
did not witness it; there is only one pillar of salt in Israel, after all. Then,
they scramble up a mountain above another town Zoar that was supposedly
safe. Their father is unconvinced of the security of this town. Therefore,
they camp in a cave facing an unknown but likely frightening future.

The rest of the story leads the reader believe that Lot did not
wake up as his first daughter left his bed. Therefore, he is too drunk to be
responsible for incest. Some of the supplementary information you provid-
ed, however, posits that this moment is potentially misinterpreted. The first
drafts in some of the earliest languages of the text are considered suspect
because of a *puncta extrordinara* over a letter. Midrash clarifies: "There is

a dot written over the letter *vav* in the word 'when she arose,' meaning that while he did not know when she lay down, he did know when she got up." Therefore, he might have expected another effort to continue the familial line after another night of drinking. Others, however, have stipulated that this *puncta* was merely a grammatical fix.

Semantics aside, these daughters stand out as rare unnamed mothers of nations. This serves to shame their action and the competing nations they bore, the Ammonites and the Moabites. By rendering an antagonist into a literary prop devoid of opinion, the focus is the insalubrious nature of the ramification of their actions, specifically competitive nations. They are both pawns and tropes while living through an extraordinary situation.

With the multiplicity of genres already represented thus far in the first chapter, there is an opportunity to develop a rape memoir. This is unfortunately a universal story. While this may be an untraditional approach the intention is to grasp a wider audience by including the thoughts and feelings of half of it.

Interpretation of this portion of the text, however, is not only the preserve of men behind official walls and their promotion of this narrative. This story has captured the attention of patrons and artists for the whole of art history. Perhaps this is why Orazio Gentileschi's traditional interpretation of *Lot and His Daughters* was actually attributed to him. Gentileschi's daughter's, with a participating Lot and his daughters looking out over an uncertain world, was long assigned to a lesser artist. The former is in Los Angeles at the Getty and the latter is in Toledo. Hanging on a wall in Ohio, her work has since been restored to her name, Artemisia Gentileschi.

Her opposing view of Lot's participation is possible because of this lack of clarity in your text. An educated young woman in Renaissance Florence, she was well steeped in your work. Her family's livelihood depended on it, after all. Additionally, at the epicenter of humanistic thought, she was likely exposed to a variety of both sacred and profane opinions. Yet, Ms. Gentileschi's greater fame and infamy lays in *Judith and Holfernes*, still consigned to a poorly lit corner of Florence's Uffizi at the behest of a horrified patroness. Your chapter, "Judith," is noted to inspire confidence: You have exhibited potential for female character development.

In Gentileschi's era, the canvases brushed by masters that replaced tatty tapestries were not only meant to keep the ominous eastern and northern winds you describe out of stony churches. With their faces painted into the story and privy to a *sacra conversazione*, the family that paid to keep the churches decorated with the ethos of the time were elevated. History is written and imagined by the victors, after all.

Those same patrons with the money to commission art were also the financiers of translations of your manuscript into the vernacular. Some dared to add chapters that were long dismissed before these translations, called Apocrypha. Some of these books were cross referenced in your text but missing in official publication for eons.

Concerning Lot and his daughters, for example, there are a few controversial additions to the story. This was described in the Book of Jasher referred to in your text, but not included. According to both an accepted medieval Midrash that retells the missing book and the interpretations of that text in translation which was dismissed as a jailable fraud, Lot had already lost a daughter. Her name was Paltith. In Sodom, it was declared a crime to feed a certain homeless wanderer. An example human decency, she fed the man. She was caught. As a result, Paltith was executed by bees.

These reclaimed Apocrypha, lost scrolls, and unsanctioned publications were previously hidden by editors that preferred a more limited publication. They focused primarily on art books then called illuminated manuscripts. In time, the rights to the work were diversified and they were translated, uncovered, and printed for all. Additionally, some kings translated from a variety of previous translations to conform the text to his own agenda, like in England. In that case, splitting hairs led to splitting necks.

Furthermore, stories from your initial chapter "Genesis" are similar to many other origin stories. Your supporters are correct in stating that the story is universal. This sentiment, however, has resulted in this text being used for political objectives. As a result, some groups are pushed to the margins because they can be related to shameful moments. For example, the Romani became "Gypsies" and the retelling of their origin story to an Irish monk on his way to a Crusade was conflated with the murderous familial dynamic between Cain and Abel found in your sample chapter,

"Genesis."

Only because your manuscript arrived with so many commendations, I would suggest further work on this book and an updated manuscript. A story that is more inclusive will logically yield a wider audience. This being said, the workshopping that has transpired over the millennia, however, has made the first manuscripts cult classics, in the original sense of the word. The amount of footnoting over thousands of years likens it to a Kinbotean analysis of John Shade's poem in Nabakov's *Pale Fire*. The story is universal because of this ability to be interpreted.

This manuscript can be defined in literary terms as a result of this atelier across the ages. An elevator pitch might be: Essentially, this work is a series of interrelated but discontinuous multi-genre vignettes describing the birth of a nation. The supplementary analysis of the original manuscript has turned that small group from a desert into a universal set of heroes and anti-heroes, permeating societal discourse for eons for an entire planet. The genre is experimental, ranging from a family epic to flashes of poetry. It is interwoven with a stream of consciousness style and the raw recounting of a traumatic rupture, inherent to memoir. There is a slave narrative that serves as a history lesson revealing the political and societal norms of that epoch. Extraordinarily, one chapter creates a genre—Proverbs. A constantly shifting narrator and a focus on the otherworldly are hints of magical realism, creating what is either utopia or dystopia, depending on the reader. Of note, the author or authors request anonymity rendering the work itself objective and untarnished by a readership's preconceived notions.

Before the elevator doors open, you should fully expect to hear my critique repeated. This already published manuscript has influenced society for millennia, but the glaring hole is the omission of half of humankind. Continuously, through multiple interpretations and translations, women suffer the burden of shame, from the opening chapter. They are given very little agency in explaining this original sin or much else. This paucity of female character development precludes this text from current publication. The story line is tested, but incomplete.

If you wish to readdress your work, your task is mighty. This work has been debated and manipulated across the millennium. Chapters are lost or discarded and have been later reprinted or rejected. The work has suffered from overediting. Some of those editors have exerted their own styles and agendas. Additionally, the order in which this work is presented feels as if it were rearranged without any further editing, creating a stilted flow. This is not the only readability issue. Crucially, many important details are lost in layers and layers of translations.

As you workshop, my best suggestion is to ask journalistic questions. Interview your unnamed and missing characters. They can create a larger, more inclusive picture, if you dare to include them. The absence of their testimony, frankly, is suspect. Ask who they knew, what they saw, why they acted as they did, where they were, and how did they feel.

Best of luck with your endeavors. Although my agency is unwilling to accept your manuscript for representation, this does not mean that your work is not inspired or powerful. At this moment, it does not fit our list.

Sincerely,
Marcella St. Denis
Agent and Founder, MSD Literary Agency

The Workman Way

Fred Pierre

Every month I struggle to balance my budget. I'd love to buy a pair of shoes, repair the car's muffler, or to take my kids to the dentist. Not everything can happen at once, so when PBS airs free financial advice during their pledge drive, I'm on it.

Last time 'round, I pledged my attention to Lucy Workman's Financial Resolutions. She was talking about one of her favorite ways to save money; bringing a sack lunch to work. "For millennials who don't have a big budget, you can save a lot by packing a lunch." It sounded like I could take a sweet vacation just by packing a lunch.

I figured that I spend four to six dollars on a bag lunch each day, or about thirteen-hundred dollars a year. Lunch at the bistro is $7.50 to go, so I'm saving around $2.50 per day times 250 days in the work year. That's six-hundred, twenty-five dollars! That ought to cover a road trip to Chicago, if we camp on the way.

I'll admit, Lucy wormed her way into my brain, and now I bring a sack lunch to work every day. Keep your brown bag though; I like it insulated, with extra compartments.

I've always had a love / hate relationship with barbers. I love them as people, but fear them as artists. When they get creative with my hair, I'm often unhappy with the results. A quality haircut is expensive. The style mavens at Colorz charge a cool fifteen – more if you want extras, and the Lou Reed look-alike charges twelve for buzz cut, but Lucy Workman has a plan for this. Lucy says avoid the high-price salon and head over to Cheap Cuts. I gave it a shot, but the quick cut missed some spots. I had to make adjustments. My wife gifted me with a sharp pair of scissors and I cleaned up my bangs. Then I trimmed around my ears. I began to feel the raw power all barbers must feel. Cutting my hair was both fun and frugal!

My first haircut was super short. I wore a cap because my head felt chilly. It quickly became a point of contention with the Director, who informed me that, "Caps are in bad taste." Since then, I've learned to cut by feel, and to feather. I understand the contours of my head and trim with the flow of my hair. My advice for newbies is to be aware that sharp scissors snip right through soft ears, so bend your earflaps back for chrissakes! I don't want to be responsible for a bloodbath.

My hair grows fast, I figure I've saved around $150 this year on trims. The key is to have two mirrors that face each other, so you can see the back of your head. Cut slowly, 'cuz you can't put hair back. It may reassure you to know that the worst mistakes grow out in less than a month!

Lucy says we're too concerned with creature comforts. We'll pay anything for TV, but won't invest a dime in our carbon-free future. She looks serious when she says that cutting my cable service will secure my financial future. It's her hardest sell, because everybody has something they like to watch. When I suggested Lucy's cable-cutting plan to my family their response was eviscerating. I asked myself, "What would Lucy do?" and I think I've found a solution.

If you want to keep your cable subscription, start a compost pile. The Garden Center stocks topsoil stripped from a foreclosed farm, but you need a lot of bags, and costs add up quickly. Compost, on the other hand, is free! Food waste turns into soil quite magically, and the secret is worms! Worms convert your food waste into nutritious soil. Recycling my yard's organic matter feels like the foundation for self-reliance. When I see neighbors rake their leaves to the curb for municipal pickup, I feel a vague sense of loss.

Drinking coffee is a sin in the church of Lucy. "You are peeing $1 million down the drain," is one of her favorite lines. Lucy goes after the coffee drinkers with ultimate sanction. I worked the numbers, and I spend around two hundred bucks a year on coffee. If I invest that in coffee stocks, with an average of 3% annual growth, I will have a million dollars in 168 years!

So armchair scientists, I ask you, what percentage of my coffee savings do I need to donate toward longevity research?

The Lucy plan is about austerity – that mysterious self-denial that afflicts so many Europeans. Austerity means not getting everything you want. It's a very un-American concept, and one that has never been fully implemented here. As much as I resent Lucy Workman telling me how to save $20 a week when I'm in debt up to my eyeballs, I follow her plan slavishly. After all, $20 is $20. As Lucy points out, you can't argue with the bottom line!

Lucy tells the story of how she got her start selling vacuum cleaners on the home shopping network. When her vacuum cleaner patent was challenged, she sued to keep her business, but the judge rejected her claim. She lost everything. You're probably asking why I listen to financial advice from someone who lost her investors $50,000. It's because Lucy always fails up!

When her vacuum cleaner startup failed, she signed up for law school. Within six months she had her degree, and went to work for a large Manhattan law firm. The firm was heavy on male attorneys and she heard a lot of "Honey, let me explain that law." When a senior attorney stole a case she'd been working on for months, she sued her own firm and won enough to pay off her vacuum cleaner investors. The experience soured her on the law, and she decided to go into multi-level marketing, with herself as the product. Patents can be challenged, but financial advice is sacrosanct, given proper disclaimers.

Lucy's courage is inspiring. She wed her partner Megan a decade before the state of New York recognized their betrothal. She's consistently advocated for the right to marry whom you choose. Some say it was her text messages that convinced the president to expire the Defense of Marriage. In an endearing proclamation, Lucy said she'd pick her love for her wife over her fortune any day, because she would "make the money back in less than three years."

Lucy recommends that everyone wargame their retirement. After all, who wants to work a sixty-hour week when you're seventy-five? Lucy Workman proves you can have it all. She even bought her own island, and to thank her fans, she's invited us to share in her success. Island stays are dirt cheap, if you attend the Workman Way weekend workshop.

I've paid into my retirement plan for ten years, and I've saved up enough for a six-month retirement, so I'm taking Lucy's advice to heart. I'll hold my investments and wait. I expect that with medical advances, I'll feel quite spry at one-hundred. Maybe I won't retire until a hundred-twenty to be on the safe side. If humans upload to the cloud, I'll need money for the electric bills. I wouldn't want my personality to get archived.

 The core message of Lucy's plan is tough love. Her voice becomes ominous when she pits pleasure today against future gratification. Lucy insists that you tell your kids "No," and explain to them that you are saving up for the future.

Makes sense, but what if you flip the script? Spend the money now, and have fun while you're young. The kids will thank you for keepin' it real. Heck, you might even stay young! Everyone benefits from some leisure.

Lucy is pointing out how self-indulgent we are, but when she extends her arm and waggles her finger, I feel like she's staring right through me. "Damn it Lucy, it was just a cup of coffee! One freaking cup." Belittling doesn't motivate me like it used to.

At first listen, Lucy sounds like a capitalist, but between the lines I hear a socialist message. It's when she starts talking about us poor working stiffs, about our lunches and loans, and how we reclaim our power through planning. She feels our pain, and that's why I trust her. She was like us until, in her wisdom, she developed the Workman Way.

Lucy advises skepticism when taking out loans, and warns us not to use credit to stave off financial ruin. It sounds to me like she's advising a profoundly anti-capitalist plan to take back our financial power. Reject mass-market materialism and focus on financial fundamentals. It's the recipe for a resilient future. Cut up your credit cards today!

I'm reading the fine print on my credit card bill. It says that if I make the minimum payment every month, I'll pay off my debt in eighteen years, if I don't charge anything new, but in my mind, I'm already buying space-proof shoes for Mars.

Lucy says stop your fear of financial predation. For your dreams to come true, repeat the mantra, "Hard Times ain't gonna rule my mind." I hear "The Secret." Lucy asks us to confront financial reality with a "What me Worry?" attitude. May I suggest that panic is motivating? Let's get real. How much of a second forty can I do? I take the bills out with some well-placed shots. Bam, the water bill, bam, the cable, bam, the property tax. All it takes is some hustle. But dammit, I'm outta cash and need coffee!

The last couple pledge drives I haven't seen Lucy. I hear she's working with Oprah. Did you get her invitation to The Workman Way series? It's all over my feed, "Break down your budget and reshape your future!"

I've made a spreadsheet to compare the course costs with its benefits. So far I'm not getting a positive answer.

The Six Grandfathers

Image by Eric Walker

Poetry by Isobel Rossiter

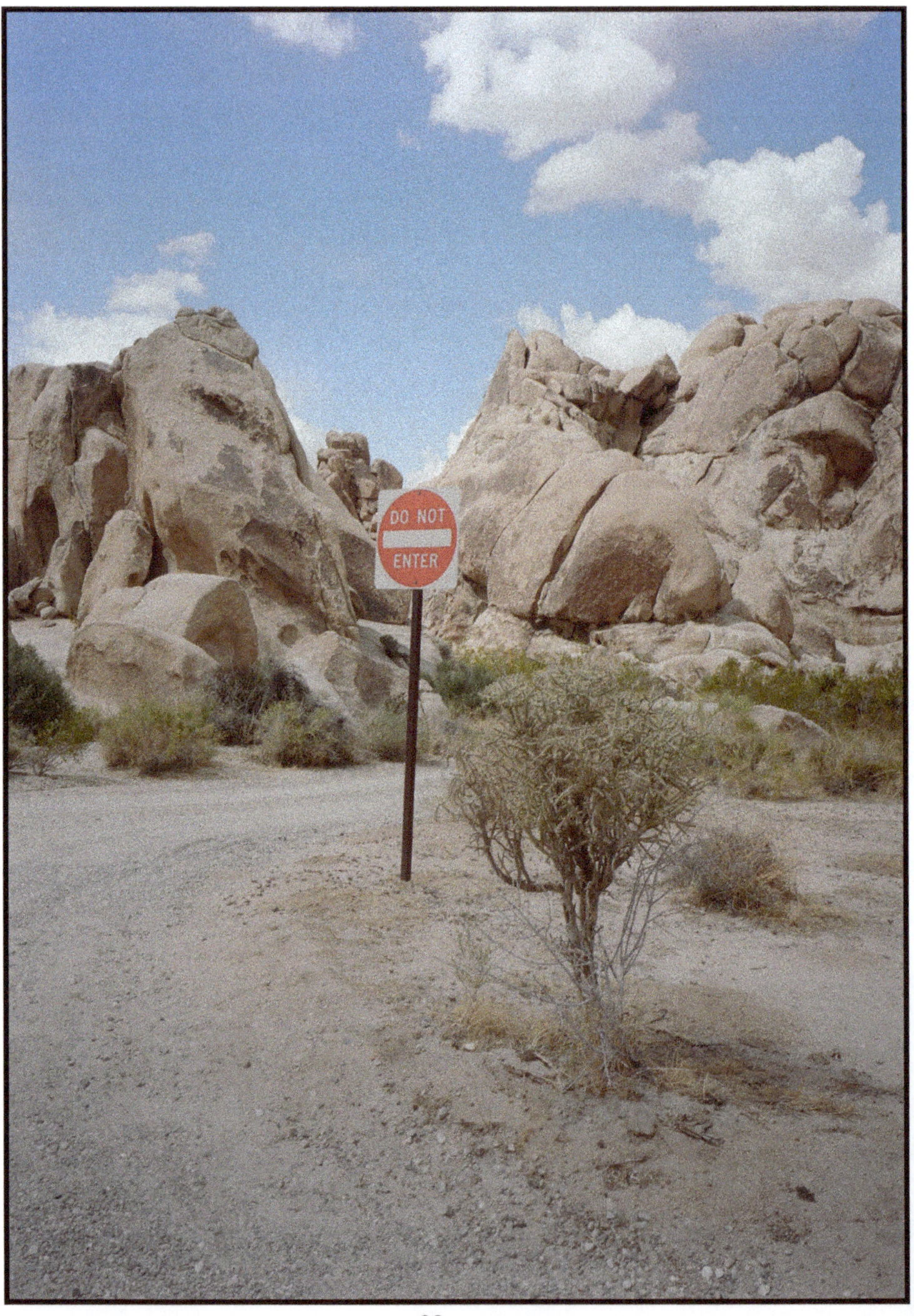

Sore scorpion side of a desert light,
Bare skeleton on its back in the sun,
And the rich dust, fur-blushed as lion hide
Bare, smooth red rock way down to grit undone
Where terse roots and stern shoots cling to dry ground
And wild tumbleweed silk is by wind spun.
Turn chin skyward and breathe moistureless clouds;
They have borne their children here from the sea.
Swallow sand-rind coating throat of the drowned
Men, grown as bloated as the bourgeoisie
That claimed their space and erected a sign:
"DO NOT ENTER – These wilds belong to me."

In Order Of Appearance:

Mitch Rayes is a second generation Lebanese-Irish american from Detroit, based in Albuquerque. Website: mitchrayes.com

For 30 years, Jamie was convinced she was bad at life. It wasn't until she learned that she is a highly sensitive person with an INFJ personality that she realized she was just bad at everyone else's lives. This moment of clarity set into motion a series of events that led to a whole new awareness of herself, the human condition, life, what lies beyond... and the abstractions began. In wave of inspiration, the marks started flowing. She was suddenly unafraid and felt everything that had been stirring inside of her begin to flow onto the canvas. The colors, the mediums, the textures and lines; they were calling to her. Jamie's intense internal reaction to color has made it one of the most important aspects of these paintings. She mixes new colors from old creating a complex and unique quality in each one-of-a-kind abstraction. Over time she has come to recognize this voice that call to her as she paints as 'source'. "These paintings are no longer mine, I am only a conduit meant to give this energy a tangible form for people to interact with." For those who are ready, these paintings offer a transformative experience. @jamieparksartist

iumi/artist, dancer, mime, actor and poet whose work is a reflection of my multi-faceted way of experiencing the world.
iumirichardcrow

George L Stein is a writer and photographer in the New Jersey/New York metropolitan area with interest in monochrome, film and digital photography, urban and rural decay, architectural, street, and more generally, art photography and digital manipulation. His work has been published in Midwest Gothic, NUNUM, Montana Mouthful, Out/Cast, The Fredericksburg Literary and Art Review, and DarkSide magazine.
instagram @steincapitalmgmt

Saleem was born and raised in Massachusetts and has spent many years in California. His written works are essentially experimental and often meet at the nexus of conscience and visceral utterance. The book of poems addresses our shifting thoughts, like sand that leave trail impressions never before imagined. Saleem's work has appeared in Chronogram Magazine and several anthologies including River Crossings: Voices of the Diaspora and a literary journal, Signifyin' Harlem: The Next Generation. He has read his poetry at the former Cornelia Street Café and other venues.
He is the author of Mind Sand – Selected Poems by Saleem Abdal-Khaaliq
The poems are a series of life's journey, his own and those he has observed. It is a book broken down into ten chapters: Dawn |Love |Wisdom |Reality |Mirror |Spirit |Noise |Fear |Music |Time
It moves from some early writings toward the vastness of lessons from experience and inner reflection. The works are often drawings, even pictures of feelings invoked by how one sees and interprets them. Poetry is often about the spaces that are left unsaid, the gap between meaning and spoken-ness. Come to this work as a passenger and be transported. A trip you won't want to miss, a world to be explored through the lens of Saleem Abdal-Khaaliq's poetry.

When not teaching, Devon Balwit sets her hand to the plough and chases chickens in Portland, OR. Her most recent chapbook is Rubbing Shoulders with the Greats [Seven Kitchens Press, 2020]. Her most recent collection is Dog-Walking in the Shadow of Pyongyang [Nixes Mate Books, 2021]. She has been an ekphrastic winner here at High Shelf.

As a world mixed media artist, PlantaRaieVilar's present imagery forms a series entitled "The Transparent Self". This theme becomes the concept vehicle that she uses to create a personal mythology of her work and the experiences that influence it. This mythology is based on a series of reenactments that mirror and embody the conflict and resolution of this emotional and aesthetic process rendered through large-scaled, up to, 10' x 10' mixed media painted- drawings on canvas or paperboard.

Anthony J. Dennis is an author, lawyer, poet and human rights activist. His poetry has appeared in a variety of literary magazines over the years including, most recently, Sheila Na Gig (Volume 5.1, Fall, 2020), Into the Void (Issue 16 - August, 2020), Dreamers (Issue 6 – July-October, 2020), Panoply (Issue 14 - January, 2020), Sons and Daughters Literary Journal (December, 2019) and The Scriblerus (Fall, 2018). He is the author of three nonfiction books and co-author of three more. Dennis holds degrees in law, literature and history from Northwestern University School of Law and Tufts University.

Andrea Lee Dunn is from Indianapolis, Indiana by way of the Texas-Mexico border and North Carolina. She studied creative writing at Texas Tech University. Examples of her work are found in New Mexico Review, Kindred Mom, Southwestern American Literature, Cagibi Journal, Entropy Magazine, the Same, and in Flying Island Literary Journal, for which she received a Pushcart Prize Nomination.
Follow her on Instagram @andrealeedunn

Grace Dilger is a poet and educator. Her work has been featured in Peach Fuzz Magazine, The Brooklyn Quarterly, The Southampton Review, Grody Mag, The Elevation Review, Proud to Be: Writing by American Warriors Vol. 9, Slug Mag, The Racket Journal, Yes, Poetry, and the forthcoming issue of Poetry City Vol. 10. She received her MFA from Stony Brook University.

Kimberly Kradel has always considered herself to be a painter – even though her first serious studies were in photography. For a long time her work was compartmentalized, her photography used for note taking and editorial work, her painting used as a force for abstractly expressing my internal thoughts and feelings.
Over time, she came to realize that she is very much a multi-disciplinary artist. Not so much because she likes to work with multiple disciplines or mixed-media within one piece, but because she likes to work with whatever materials are available to her at any given time. So her portfolio as a whole is multi-disciplinary.
Kradel seriously returned to using photography as her main form of creating art in 2007. At first it was economics that forced her hand. Now, she thinks it may have been fate, or maybe destiny, that made her return to working with light.
No matter what the medium, the common theme behind her work is her fascination with time and space. Kradel is interested in tearing through the concept of linear time and discovering new ways to use the universe as an art form. Chaos theory, moving between dimensions, and communication are also common themes in her work.

Chris Norcross is a Philadelphia based writer and musician. His work has appeared in various journals, including ICEVIEW, and Slow Time. His current project explores the peculiar, personal phenomenology of a moment.

Mac Chandler is a creative writing student at The University of the Arts in Philadelphia. Her work can be seen in Rappahannock Review, HASH Journal, and on her Instagram, @frillysox.

John Lightle is a writer and photographer spending many hours sitting on his woodpile contemplating. While away from his frame shop, he drags his artwork among many area art shows. The job takes him across the countryside, and occasionally overseas, photographing the quiet resolve found within the golden hours.

Simas is a teacher of literature currently living in Melbourne, Australia. His father was a musician, and his mother loved silence. Sam already has gray hair.

After a career in antiquarian books, N.M. Campbell expatriated from America. The author lives in an old house with a handful of antiques, a tiny kitchen, thousands of books, and a giant Maine Coon who permits people to live there.

Fred Pierre writes about the near future with a healthy mix of skepticism and optimism and goal to be honest. He weaves humor with pathos while staying on mission, to skewer our myths about money. Fred's writing is featured on Poet's Choice YouTube and on Neutral Spaces, with work forthcoming in Tiny Seed Journal. This story pokes fun at financial gurus and their overlarge egos.

Portland-based photographer/multimedia artist Eric Walker explores the vernacular of signage amongst the American West in the series 'If A Stop Sign Falls' focusing less on the literal directive of the object and more on how it shapes and informs surrounding landscapes. The work aims to hone in on the fragile border between human development and natural processes. Instagram: @edubyeah

Isobel Rossiter is a first year Creative Writing student at the University of Birmingham. Focusing primarily on poetry, her work explores her queer, national and religious identities; Rossiter is always striving towards a better understanding of the world and the people around her. Experienced in ekphrasis, she has previously created a feminist collection responding to Picasso's 'Les Demoiselles d'Avignon' in which she looked through the eyes of the artist's mistreated muses.
Having a great love for travel, influences from across the world appear in the imagery of Rossiter's poetry, as well as the apple trees and combine harvesters of her beloved home county of Somerset, UK.

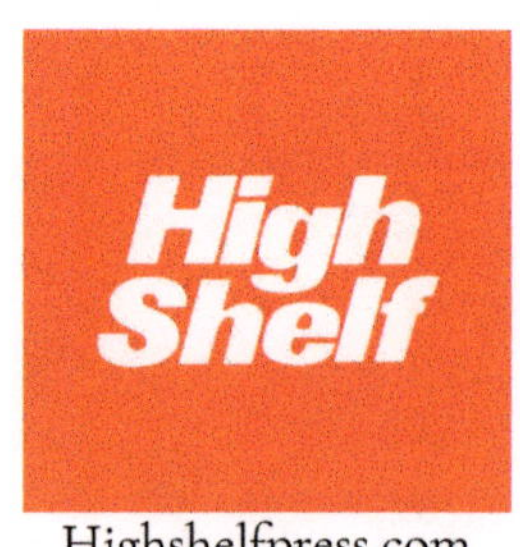

Highshelfpress.com